The Atlantic Salmon Handbook

AN ATLANTIC SALMON FEDERATION BOOK

The Atlantic Salmon Handbook

AN ATLANTIC SALMON FEDERATION BOOK

A COMPACT GUIDE TO ALL ASPECTS OF FLY FISHING FOR THE KING OF GAME FISH

PETER BODO

ILLUSTRATED BY JONATHAN MILO

The Lyons Press

Printed in the United States of America
Design and composition by Rohani Design, Edmonds, Washington

10 9 8 7 6 5 4 3 2 1

Library of Congress Cataloging-in-Publication Data

Bodo, Peter
    The Atlantic salmon handbook / Peter Bodo.
        p.   cm.
    "An Atlantic Salmon Federation book."
    Includes index.
    ISBN 1-55821-510-7(cl). ISBN 1-55821-511-5 (pb)
    1. Atlantic salmon fishing. 2. Atlantic salmon fishing—Canada.
    I. Title.
SH685.B64 1997
799.1'756'097—dc21   97-8223
                                                                      CIP

For Joseph F. Cullman III, cofounder and

chairman emeritus of the Atlantic Salmon

Federation. No fish ever had a better friend.

CONTENTS

ACKNOWLEDGMENTS

In their acknowledgments, authors generally single out individuals who helped prepare a book. So it seems a little odd for me to be starting this page with the name of an institution, the Atlantic Salmon Federation. But then I don't think of the ASF as only a conservation organization fighting the good fight—I also consider it a collection of friends and acquaintances with whom I share a deep sense of solidarity, and for whom I feel great personal warmth.

I've been a member of the ASF for many years, and I currently serve on its U.S. National Council. The ASF helped shape my way of thinking about salmon and salmon fishing, and it provided invaluable help in the conception and execution of this project. In addition to Joe Cullman, to whom this book is dedicated, I'd also like to single out for thanks the current ASF president (and fishing buddy), Bill Taylor, as well as the organization's two chairmen, Lucien G. Rolland (ASF Canada) and Donal C. O'Brien Jr. (ASF U.S.). Sue Scott, the ASF's director of communications, and Harry Bruce, the former editor of the *Atlantic Salmon Journal,* also helped this project come to fruition.

Nick Lyons, a formidable author and the publisher of this book, revealed himself as a real friend of the salmon conservation movement by taking on this project. Jim Emery, a friend, fishing companion, and ardent student of salmon literature, graciously suffered through his role as my test reader. From deep in his bunker in Searsport, Maine, editor James R. Babb took a manuscript and turned it into this book.

A special thanks to past and present salmon fishing buddies: Paul Nevin, Chris and Rudy von Strasser, Bill George, Richard Franklin, Greg Hubert, Isabelle Fritz-Cope, Bill McHenry, George Semler, David Taylor, Bart and Ned Hayes, Jim Guinta, Tim Sullivan, and Wayne Norderg. Many of these anglers fished with me at Maclennan Lodge on the Upsalquitch River in New Brunswick.

Which brings me to the individual who played the largest role in shaping me as a salmon fisherman: A. Tucker Cluett. In 1980 Cluett, whom I only knew casually through my friendship with Paul Nevin, invited us to fish with him at Maclennan Lodge. I basically stayed for two decades. Over that period, I consumed unconscionable amounts of Tucker's hootch. I ate a prodigious number of sumptuous meals prepared by Ada Thomas and her lovely daughter, Nancy. I learned vast amounts about salmon fishing and rivercraft from Tucker and three guides who instructed me in the ways of salmon—the brothers David and Shane Mann, along with Ollie Marshall. Some of that learning even stuck, which is why I was able to write this book. I can't thank you enough, Tucker.

FOREWORD

Peter Bodo has produced a book that needed to be written. Its subject—the Atlantic salmon, the greatest freshwater gamefish that swims, and where to find it—has fascinated me since early boyhood, when I had the rare privilege of spending summers at my parents' summer house overlooking the junction of the Forks with the Dartmouth River, approximately 10 miles from the town of Gaspe. Our house was almost at the end of the road, such as it was, and we were surrounded by thick evergreen forests stretching from the hilltops almost to the river's edge.

My world extended from the Forks, with its crystal-clear water harboring speckled trout behind sheltering boulders, to the deeper, dark-shadowed pools of the Dartmouth, where great Atlantic salmon rested quietly, leaning against the river's gravel-strewn bottom or lying behind ledges and larger rocks to shelter them from the current's constant pressure and hide them from their pursuers. These included Jules Timmins, a mining magnate from Montreal, who had a lodge not far upstream, and my dad, who loved to fish the pool in front of our house very early in the morning—before Mr. Timmins's river warden made his regular rounds.

You see, the river, including the part flowing by our house, was leased to Mr. Timmins by the Quebec government, and no one was permitted to fish except him and his guests. My job, as a redheaded, freckle-faced kid of eight or nine, was to position myself in the fork of a big birch tree at the head of the pool, where I had a clear, unobstructed view both upstream and down, and signal my dad when I saw the warden coming. We would then both hide in the woods until he passed. A bit later, when I was 10, I caught my first salmon there on a 12-foot bamboo smelt pole I had rigged up with guides made from the hinged ends of safety pins, a reel fastened on with rabbit wire and electrician's tape, a King Eider line, and a moth-eaten Silver Doctor fly filched from my dad's leather fishing box. I was so excited and engrossed in saving my first-ever salmon that I didn't notice the long canoe edging onto the beach at the head of the pool, discharging two burly guides and Mr. Timmins, all decked out in his plus fours and fancy fishing regalia. Trying to beach my salmon and control my excitement, I backed right into the outstretched arms of the lodge's head guide, Walter Stanley. I tried to break free from Walter's bear hug, kicking and swearing and threatening the dire consequences that would await when my dad caught up with him, but to no avail. My salmon, my rod, and I were delivered to Mr. Timmins, who had been watching the unequal contest with some amusement.

"What's your name, son?" he said.

"Wilfred Carter," I replied sullenly, on the edge of tears.

"Don't you know you can't fish here?" asked Mr. Timmins.

"I don't see why you can and my dad and I can't," I responded with stubborn 10-year-old passion.

Immediately there was a change in Mr. Timmins, and the earlier sternness left his voice. "Do you and your father live up there?" he said, pointing to our gray-shingled cottage right on the riverbank.

"Yes," I replied.

"I'd like to meet your dad," said Mr. Timmins. "Why don't the two of you come up to the lodge and fish with me on Saturday?" He turned to Walter Stanley to add, "Give Wilfred his rod and his salmon, and we'll talk about this little problem again on Saturday."

Reluctantly Walter complied, and I grabbed my precious rod and beautiful salmon and disappeared up the bank to the house like a twice-scared rabbit.

The following Saturday Dad and I met Jules Timmins at his lodge and shared a memorable day with him in his canoe. I caught my second salmon and warmed up to our host considerably when he told us that we were welcome to fish the pool in front of our house anytime it was not occupied by himself or one of his guests. Over the next 25 years, until his death, I fished frequently with Jules Timmins, as we shared thoughts on salmon conservation and fishing. He even convinced me to abandon the worms I still liked to use to entice especially large trout!

In those halcyon days of chasing trout and salmon in favorite holes on the Forks and the Dartmouth, or sometimes bagging a careless partridge, I learned quite a lot about the biology of the fish and wildlife so abundant in that beautiful part of Canada. I can still remember clearly the huge mass of trout that would move off like a giant shadow as I approached the canoe landing to cross over to Jules Timmins's lodge, and the salmon lying lazily in schools numbering in the hundreds in the pools below. The salmon especially fascinated me, and I was determined to find out everything I could about them—where they came from, why they didn't seem to eat, why they would sometimes attack a fly ferociously and other times ignore it, and where they went when the rivers froze over in the winter.

After a stint with the Canadian army in Europe as a teenage soldier and then the earning of a degree in biology, I ended up working for the government of Quebec. Eventually I was responsible for fish and wildlife management on the Gaspe Peninsula and the Quebec North Shore, an area about as big as Texas and harboring some of the greatest salmon rivers in the world.

While at times preoccupied with problems affecting deer, moose, and other wildlife, I always managed to find time to pursue my special interest in salmon. The gamefish had engulfed me in a serious love affair from which I have never recovered.

That interest in salmon and salmon rivers brought me into contact with a great many people who just liked to fish for salmon, and a few who shared my concern for the struggle the fish seemed to be having to survive and prosper in a time when industry was expanding, land-based resources were being heavily exploited, and fishing boats with ever-bigger nets were multiplying rapidly wherever there was anything to catch in the world's oceans. Whenever we met our discussions turned eventually to why the government didn't really seem to care what happened to the salmon, and what could be done to save those magnificent creatures from following the pattern of most European and northeastern American rivers, where the salmon had disappeared entirely.

In 1968 I was living in Gaspe with my wife, Pauline, and our children, working hard and enjoying my career, with frequent excursions to favorite pools on the Dartmouth, York, Ste. Jean, Bonaventure, Grand Cascapedia, Matane, Moisie, Natashquan, and other rivers. One day two visitors were announced—Francis Goelet and B. E. Ted Bensinger, both salmon fishermen who owned fishing lodges on the famous Restigouche River. They wanted to discuss an idea they had about forming an organization to promote conservation and better management of Atlantic salmon. They said that they had other friends and associates who shared their concern about the salmon and wanted to help, too; all were prepared to contribute to the financing of the new organization if I would come aboard as the founding executive director!

After several more meetings and planning and many hours of anxious discussion with friends and family I decided to take the plunge, and headed off to New York to meet with some of the others involved in the new venture. That's when the International Atlantic Salmon Foundation (IASF) was born, and that's when I first met Joseph F. Cullman III, who was later to succeed Francis Goelet as president and become my mentor and cherished friend.

Joe was at that time chairman and CEO of the huge Philip Morris, Inc.; in his free time he played golf and tennis, and fished for salmon at Runnymede, his lodge on the Restigouche, as well as at Two Brooks Lodge on the Upsalquitch, which he shared with Ted Bensinger. Joe was a busy, hard-working executive who traveled extensively on business or to pursue his other deep and abiding interest—conservation. He was then a trustee of the World Wildlife Fund U.S., and had been a moving force in getting the U.S. arm of this prestigious conservation organization going. He was also very interested in the plight of wildlife in Africa, giving generously to support worthy conservation efforts by the WWF and other organizations. But his most passionate love affair was with Atlantic salmon.

One day when we were sharing a canoe on the Restigouche, Joe told me jokingly that he probably had some Atlantic salmon genes coursing through his blood, because his mother had told him that he was conceived on the banks of the Ste. Marguerite River one gorgeous summer day when the salmon fishing was indifferent and his parents found something more exciting to do! His mother, he said, called him "her salmon-pink baby." Indeed, Joe's dedication and devotion to Atlantic salmon conservation and his love of salmon fishing are so deeply ingrained that he surely must have a few of *Salmo salar*'s genes in his bloodstream.

Joe steered the IASF through some very difficult times and supported me unfailingly as we worked to build a strong and effective salmon conservation constituency. The salmon's world was changing and we were leading the charge to save it from the insatiable greed of commercial fishermen and indifference of government bureaucrats.

Our first major challenge was to find a way to control the Greenland driftnet fishery, which was then catching as many as 600,000 salmon every year, at least half of them hatched in the rivers of Canada and New England. The IASF, under Joe's leadership and generous financial support, led a coalition of conservation organizations in a campaign that ended with a ban on the distant high-seas fishery off Greenland and an annual quota on the inshore take by local fishermen. That was a conservation watershed, because without those controls the Atlantic salmon would have faced certain extinction.

Joe Cullman was also a key player in the drive to unite the International Atlantic Salmon Foundation with the Atlantic Salmon Association (ASA), and in January 1982 these two leading salmon conservation organizations united as the Atlantic Salmon Federation (ASF). The federation moved quickly to bring many local and regional salmon conservation groups under its umbrella, establishing a number of regional councils comprised of local, grassroots salmon conservation organizations. The ASF became the largest and most articulate and effective private-sector conservation organization dedicated to the conservation and management of Atlantic salmon throughout the North Atlantic. In the years ahead the ASF was to lead many conservation initiatives in international cooperation, education, research, and management of Atlantic salmon.

Perhaps the most significant achievement during that period, and one that would not have happened without the courageous and tenacious support Joe gave me, was the ASF's leadership role in establishing the salmon aquaculture industry as the quickest and best way to remove the commercial fishery for wild salmon in the sea. The ASF directors were divided on this issue—some pushing strongly for a declaration of the salmon as a gamefish, others supporting my view that such a declaration would accomplish nothing more than to pit the ASF against governments and commercial fishermen in a bitter public and media squabble. In the end Joe's great credibility and strong leadership gained me the support we needed, and the ASF planted its support firmly behind salmon aquaculture as the best way to provide salmon for the marketplace and to remove the market for wild-caught salmon. That strategy proved correct. Today there remain only limited commercial salmon fisheries in Greenland, Labrador, and the United Kingdom. Thousands of nets have been removed from the water and are no longer strangling Atlantic salmon on their annual migrations.

But that is only part of the ASF conservation story. The federation's most significant contribution over time may be the catalyst role it played in both enrolling thousands of individuals in the salmon conservation crusade and convincing governments that a resource so precious deserved better stewardship. Today there is a virtual army of salmon conservation supporters around the North Atlantic speaking out and taking action on behalf of the beleaguered salmon.

The role Joe Cullman, to whom this book is dedicated, played in the salmon conservation drama cannot be overstated. The support he gave to me over the years was extraordinary, and I treasure the close friendship that grew through our shared concern for the Atlantic salmon's plight. It will endure as long as the rivers run and the salmon return home.

Fishing for Atlantic salmon has changed dramatically during my lifetime, and I think that the broad grassroots constituency created by the ASF has had a lot to do with it. There are still privately owned fishing rights on some parts of rivers in Quebec and New Brunswick, but most rivers are now partly or entirely available for public fishing. Some are under the control of local management associations (ZECs); others are administered by outfitters who provide fishing and accommodations; in some areas government agencies allow only resident fishing under daily permits, and in others all that is required is a fishing license and the ability to access the river.

This maze of salmon fishing possibilities has evolved in response to an ever-growing interest in salmon fishing. To the novice the sport is often intimidating and confusing. Peter Bodo's book will now make it much easier for fishers to find out where to go, how to get there, and what to expect after arriving. The descriptions of rivers, what kind of fishing to expect, seasons, limits, licenses, and whom to contact for necessary permits and arrangements will clear away much of the confusion and frustration many aspiring salmon fishers have experienced; and the practical information on tactics, flies, and how to fight fish will be very helpful. *The Atlantic Salmon Handbook* is truly a book whose time has come; it should be an indispensable piece of every salmon fisher's equipment. Don't leave home without it.

—Wilfred M. Carter
1997

INTRODUCTION

The traditional image of Atlantic salmon fishing wells up from one of those ubiquitous Ogden Pleissner watercolors, where it is always foggy, a teakettle is always steaming on the rocky bank, and a salmon—"the king of gamefish, the gamefish of kings"—is always leaping in the mist at the end of a long line. This scene is usually played out on a private river that you will never fish, no matter how much money you have.

Salmon fishing is also awash in a fair amount of mumbo-jumbo about fly patterns, including pseudoscientific "color theories" about fly-tying materials and their effects on salmon. The challenge of inducing a salmon to take a fly has generated some pretty wild angling techniques, and all have worked. At least once.

In salmon fishing every old chestnut ("Bright day, bright fly; dark day, dark fly," for instance, or "Blue flies don't work in Canada") can be blown to smithereens on the battleground of experience, and every blowhard can wear the mantle of expertise until the next genius yanks it off. The fundamental tenet of salmon fishing is that no theory can be conclusively proved—or disproved. And the fundamental charm of salmon fishing is the mysterious, unpredictable nature of this great fish.

But despite the elitist patina and esoteric nature of the sport, salmon fishing in North America is no longer a pastime reserved for the rich, nor is it a particularly daunting challenge for an angler of reasonable experience and skill.

Don't get me wrong. I'm fond of Pleissner prints. I also like fully dressed featherwing salmon flies, waxed-cotton raincoats, fine cane rods, and Bogdan and Vom Hofe reels. That is, I like *looking* at them, anyway. And just as advances in metal and graphite technologies have changed those once sensible fishing tools—a double-handed cane rod and a hand-crafted Bogdan reel—into charming affectations, so sweeping changes in public policy and environmental conditions over the past 25 years have changed the face of salmon fishing in North America.

Some of the rivers immortalized by Pleissner are still largely controlled by individuals or groups who pay extravagant sums for exclusive fishing rights. But almost every one of those rivers offers *some* public water, although getting to fish it often depends on the pure luck of a lottery draw. And many fine salmon rivers in eastern Canada are entirely, or almost entirely, managed for public fishing.

The competition to get on prime stretches of those rivers can also be fierce, but this is due more to conservation policy than to social policy. The essence of conservation is maintaining a sensible balance between exploiting and protecting a limited, precious resource. In most places free and unlimited salmon fishing—similar to what trout fishers enjoy after paying a nominal license fee—simply cannot be justified if conservation concerns are considered. Nevertheless, more salmon rivers are now accessible to more "typical" anglers than ever before.

My fishing buddy Jim Emery, a contemporary jazz guitarist and composer, is the best fisherman I know, probably because his ever-increasing stores of knowledge and experience have *never* diminished or corrupted his boyish enthusiasm for catching fish. Jim's sharp eyesight, excellent eye-hand coordination, strength, and concentration, combined with his appetite for knowledge, make him the ultimate fisherman.

In July 1991, on a 13-day fishing trip, Jim hooked 21 salmon and landed 15, including a 24-pound male and a henfish of 18 pounds. And he did this on the upper Matapedia, probably the most widely known and heavily fished public salmon water in Quebec.

Okay, 1991 was a very good year throughout eastern Canada. And Jim, who had booked his fishing dates seven months earlier, was very lucky to catch the river in perfect condition. Of course *you should never discount the value of good timing and good luck;* both are inherent rules of salmon fishing. But many other fishermen were on the river those same two weeks who never hooked a salmon.

Jim rarely fishes for salmon anywhere but the Matapedia. A realist who prefers familiarity to adventure and certitude to risk, he isn't about to waste the few days he can fish each year stumbling around a river he doesn't know. This brings up another rule of salmon fishing: *Familiarity is the most potent ingredient in salmon fishing success* (more on this in chapter 6).

Jim got skunked on his first salmon fishing foray, in 1987, but between 1988 and 1996 he hooked 81 salmon on the Matapedia and landed 61. These are outstanding numbers that quantify the kind of fishing a skilled, dedicated angler can find on a river open to anyone with a valid license or, in some cases, day permit (see appendix I for a comprehensive listing of fees and regulations).

The Matapedia is neither remote nor pristine and provides little in the way of solitude or adventure. But it is a prolific salmon river with a distinguished history, a great deal of which is preserved in the restored Matamajaw Salmon Club lodge in the town of Causapscal. It has been celebrated in dozens of prized angling prints. It's the home river of the legendary guide Richard Adams. And the fishing is as available as sliced bread.

But there's another way to become a salmon angler besides concentrating on one river until you know it intimately—the one I chose when I took my first trip to Quebec in 1983. At the weekly luncheons of New York's Theodore Gordon Flyfishers, my lifelong fishing friend Richard Franklin and I met Chris von Strasser. Chris had just returned from a month of bumming around on Quebec's Gaspe Peninsula with his friend Bill George. Although Chris had both the means and social contacts to secure excellent fishing on private water, he wanted to catch his salmon the hard and glorious way—by exploring the rivers the Quebec government had reclaimed from private owners and opened to public fishing during the 1970s.

Chris's tales and photos convinced Richard and me—two kids who had grown up in the suburbs of New York and cut our fishing teeth on killies, bluegills, and stocked trout in municipal ponds—that we *had* to fish the Gaspe Peninsula for "the king of gamefish."

The following July, Richard and I planned a two-week trip that would take us to Gaspe rivers as far-flung as the Ste. Anne, a north-flowing jewel that enters the Gulf of Saint Lawrence at the picturesque village of Ste. Anne-des-Monts. By then Richard and I had fished and camped our way through the great trout fishing regions of Montana and parts of Idaho. We had read up on Atlantic salmon, bought or tied dozens of salmon flies, and picked the brains of every salmon angler we could find.

Our first evening we camped at a lovely spot overlooking the Saint Lawrence, built a fire, ate, and drank a few Scotches. It had rained heavily earlier that day, and we knew that a rise of water always brought fresh fish into the rivers. Shortly before we turned in Richard stood up, lifted his plastic tumbler of Scotch, and, wobbling slightly, said, "Peter, I have a feeling that we're going to catch big fish, and lots of 'em."

Big fish and lots of 'em.

To this day I remember the empty feeling that spread through the pit of my stomach even before Richard finished his sentence. I felt that we were in big trouble, and lots of it.

For the next two weeks we fished and drove through wild, rugged country. It was nearly 10 miles one way from our dilapidated hotel to the nearest coffee stop, then some 25 miles the other way, mostly over a twisting, rutted logging road, to the pools of the Ste. Anne. After a morning's fishing we drove another 20 miles to a highway pay phone to get fishing permits for the following day. Then it was back to the river for the afternoon and evening fishing. By the time we got off the river and back to town it was often after 11 P.M.—and there was noplace open to eat. We lived on cheese-filled crackers and pop from a vending machine. At five each morning it began all over again. Most of the time it was sunny and hot, and the water was very low. Obviously, Mr. Pleissner hadn't spent much time in *this* neck of the woods.

I caught exactly two fish, both grilse of under 4 pounds, one on the Ste. Anne and the other on the Petite Cascapedia. Richard hooked and lost one grilse on the Ste. Anne. That was it.

Playing a large Atlantic salmon on light tackle is one of the most exciting experiences in all angling (Photo: Val Atkinson)

Nevertheless I fell in love with salmon fishing on that hard, exhausting trip. Sometimes I wonder if that would have happened if we had indeed caught "big fish and lots of 'em." Something about the rugged, isolated Gaspe addressed a part of me that was tired of gung-ho trout fishers in cowboy hats, geeky bug experts, and discontented schoolteachers who had fled suburban lives to reinvent themselves as western fishing guides.

On the Gaspe we fished isolated rivers that were of unparalleled beauty even when nothing was in them. I would fall asleep, exhausted, on the rocky riverbank and awake to a chill breeze and molten afternoon light that was beyond lonesome. On the odd occasions when we did manage to get a hot shower or a good meal in a roadside diner, our joy was profound. We encountered few other fishermen and saw just enough fish—some in the rivers, a few in the possession of thrilled anglers—to keep us focused and me captivated.

I fished the Matapedia and other rivers for a year or two afterward, then my friend Paul Nevin and I were invited to fish at Maclennan Lodge, a private camp owned by a family friend of the Nevins, A. Tucker

Cluett. At Tucker's we fished prime, storied water from graceful canoes with the best and most expert of guides. We ate sumptuous meals, and while we were fishing, our beds were made and our laundry washed. With that experience my introduction to salmon fishing was complete, although my education continues.

A few paragraphs ago I wrote that I fell in love with salmon "fishing." Any fisherman—make that any human being with a sense of aesthetics—*has* to love the Atlantic salmon. Heck, I loved them long before I caught one.

But loving a fish and loving a kind of fishing are entirely different. The bluefin tuna is a stunning fish whose beauty looks almost engineered, but I don't care for the way it's caught, with heavy terminal tackle on rolling seas. I love trout, but in many of the best places trout fishing has become a matter of ultrafine leaders, microscopic flies, and the intense concentration of a miniaturist painter. By contrast, the salmon angler is an abstract expressionist who works instinctively on a large canvas, with simple, sturdy tools.

In this book I'll describe the unique techniques and traditions of salmon fishing and try to explain just how this sport can be simultaneously a science and a crapshoot, grand and zany, inspiring and heartbreaking. I'd like to think that should you decide to go salmon fishing, you can throw this book in your duffel bag and have a good shot at success without having to read anything else. And if this book makes you want to try salmon fishing, all the better.

CHAPTER 1

This Unique Fish

I'll assume that most readers of this book have some knowledge of fly fishing and that they, like most salmon anglers, began as trout fishers. Salmon are both very much like and entirely different from trout. Understanding this apparent contradiction is essential to successful salmon fishing.

Salmon and trout, both members of the Salmonid family, are similar in appearance and share many biological and behavioral traits. For this reason many new salmon anglers bring along a trout fisher's mentality. For instance, trout fishers usually overemphasize the fly's role in salmon fishing and underemphasize the importance of reading water and locating fish. To extend the analogy I made in this book's introduction, it's the difference between a miniaturist painter and an expressionist working on a big canvas.

The trout fisher's fixation on the fly is understandable, but it's important to appreciate why this isn't valid in salmon fishing. Trout prefer to live and feed in specific places and, except during spawning migrations or when river conditions become inhospitable, resist displacement from their homes, or *lies.* The best trout lies offer an optimal combination of comfort, food, and protection from predators. Biologists can easily quantify a trout stream's productivity, or *carrying capacity,* in terms of fish-per-mile statistics.

In a stream known to be productive, a trout fisher familiar with trout habitat is almost always casting over fish. He needn't move from a place that appears dead; insects may start hatching and the surface might begin to boil with feeding fish. He needn't worry that specific water conditions have concentrated fish 15 miles upstream and that the water he's on is barren. Usually a number of fish are right in front of him, most of them invisibly at rest in their habitat. Rather than go hunting for specific, visible fish, a trout angler need only await the fulfillment of certain conditions that will create opportunities to catch fish; then he needs the knowledge and skill to present the "right" fly in a realistic fashion to a feeding fish. Trout fishing is highly empirical, which is exactly why so many people love it.

Now consider salmon. After spending between two and four years in their natal rivers, they go out to sea. A certain percentage of fish in each generation (the figures vary from river to river) return to the river after spending just one winter at sea. These salmon are called *grilse,* and generally weigh 3 to 6 pounds. Most are males, and they appear to be Mother Nature's way of creating valuable overlap between generations. More than anything else, grilse ensure that an adequate number of male fish are present to service the females at spawning time.

Ironically, the greatest testament to the versatility and value of grilse is the way their numbers have virtually exploded on many heavily fished salmon rivers. An inordinately high number of grilse on a river system suggests that grilse survive natural and man-made dangers that larger salmon cannot withstand. Heaven forbid we ever see a day when only one salmon is left on earth. But if we do, that fish undoubtedly will be a grilse.

The remaining fish in any year-class remain at sea for at least two winters before returning to spawn. A typical salmon—an *MSW,* or *multi-sea-winter* fish—weighs between 8 and 12 pounds, depending on its genetic heritage and such variables as the availability of food on its high-seas feeding grounds.

The first of the three great pillars upon which successful salmon fishing rests is: *Understand the nature of the fish.* A salmon returning to its home river is strictly a visitor on a narrow mission to reproduce. It has a destination, usually the ideal spawning and nursery habitat found most often in a river's headwaters and tributaries. Although salmon generally won't spawn until October, most North American salmon begin to enter the rivers in May, before their reproductive capabilities or sexual organs are fully developed.

The salmon's urge to reproduce is not merely an instinct—as are those that motivate it to eat, escape predators, or even play or take a fly. It is a protracted, consuming process that over time obliterates all other urges and instincts. This is why North America's settlers and today's unscrupulous poachers can literally pitchfork spawning salmon off their redds. For the salmon, reproduction gradually becomes an even higher imperative than survival.

So in small but real daily increments, the fat, frisky salmon that enters a river in May or June ceases to exist. By October its bright silver flanks have turned burnished copper, and the larger male fish have developed scary-looking *kypes* (hooked lower jaws). These profound biological changes are reflected behaviorally as well. Male fish aggressively protect the female fish and the immediate territory of their redds, but show no interest in anything not directly related to spawning. Juvenile male *parr,* which are about six inches long, have been known to sneak into a redd to add a squirt of their own milt while an enormous pair of MSW salmon are otherwise engaged.

Understanding the change that salmon undergo helps explain the fish's often puzzling and unpredictable behavior. It also helps explain why, even though a determined salmon could reach good spawning habitat in many rivers in only two or three days, most summer-run salmon enter a river many months before they spawn. Think of the river as a transparent chrysalis, inside of which each fish changes over time from an athletic, aggressive feeding machine into a simple instrument of procreation.

The first readily apparent change is the loss of appetite—and you need not be an angler to understand the implications of that. Biologists agree that a salmon's digestive ability short-circuits when the fish returns to fresh water, and during the spawning run it lives off fat accumulated at sea. Occasionally you may hear or read about salmon whose stomachs are found to contain anything from baitfish to mayflies to pinecones, but these aberrations are rare.

You may wonder about the grand natural plan requiring that fish that won't spawn until the leaves turn color enter their natal rivers before some of the buds even open. But the protective spring tunnel of cold, high water shields large salmon from the dangers of late-summer, low-water conditions. These include formidable physical obstacles to passage (gravel bars, shallow riffles, impossibly tall waterfalls), increased exposure to predators, and the shock of high water temperatures on fish accustomed to the icy seas. Some of the largest salmon are often the first fish to enter the river, indicating that there is a survival advantage in doing so. They didn't get to be the biggest fish purely by chance.

Fortunately, even though salmon stop feeding they still exhibit feeding behavior for at least their first few weeks in fresh water. Exactly why salmon take a fly is one of the sport's ancient, burning mysteries. In his exhaustive book *Salmon Fishing: A Practical Guide* (Witherby, London, 1984), British author Hugh Falkus breaks down the response into six categories, listed in the order of the frequency with which they appear to account for takes:

1. Feeding habit
2. Aggression
3. Inducement
4. Curiosity
5. Irritation
6. Playfulness

Lee Wulff, the late dean of American salmon anglers, had a theory that salmon also take from "parr memory." Wulff postulated that the return to fresh water triggered in a salmon some unconscious memory of having lived there as a juvenile, feeding freely on anything that came its way. I don't know about the science, but the theory certainly is charming. And it does tie in somehow with almost all of Falkus's reasons.

Falkus's six reasons should be self-explanatory. (By "inducement," Falkus means that a fish takes a fly for the same reason that a cat chases a bug it doesn't intend to eat: It's there, and it's trying to get away.) But I want to make a few points that may not be obvious.

The *reasons* that salmon take vary more than it may appear, and the *way* they take is often a function of the reasons they take. Playfulness is a mood that has as much to do with a fish's take as does the fly, or presentation. Explosive aggression takes depend on a "trigger" (usually fly placement, style, color, or size) that elicits a sudden behavioral response—one that the fish, given the opportunity, would just as soon take back, the way we sometimes wish to take back something we've blurted out. And the most common take, the classic rise to a wet fly, is different still.

Falkus points out that the feeding habit take is "very gentle but very positive." Salmon usually take a wet fly with a measured determination that is one of the special joys of salmon fishing. As the fly swings overhead the salmon swims up from its lie, takes the fly, then turns back to its resting place. If you observe the cardinal rule of technique—*don't strike a salmon when it takes a wet fly*—what you'll feel is a sudden long, steady pull as the fish returns to its lie with the fly in his mouth. In a leisurely way, the fish sinks the hook better than you ever could with a manual strike. It's clear from the way this transpires that there's nothing reflexive, hasty, or imprudent about this process, as there is about some other kinds of takes. In taking a wet fly in the typical way, the fish is doing something customary and familiar.

I make these points to show how salmon fishing is intrinsically different from trout fishing and from most other kinds of fishing. These are the kinds of issues a salmon angler must understand and contemplate to be successful. I've had a salmon race across a pool, the white insides of its mouth clearly visible as it bore down on and eventually engulfed my tiny dry fly. I've also had fish visibly "peck" a wet fly without taking it, and take a dry fly by the hackle, without touching the steel hook. These are the experiences, challenges, and contradictions of which salmon fishing is made.

Another important thing to remember is that in a broad, foundational way, salmon are very territorial. I'm convinced that this is often the key to making them take, and the essential motive that sets in motion the process of rising to a fly. Imagine a salmon in a lie watching a strange object that appears alive coming slowly and inexorably toward it. This is exactly what happens in the traditional step-cast-step wet-fly method, whereby an angler meticulously combs a pool, covering all the water by fishing it in an orderly, repetitive way. The most successful salmon fishers are the ones with the patience—if not the preference—for fishing this way. After all, there's nothing particularly "expert" or impressive about covering a pool by repeatedly making the same cast, taking a small step after each, until you've worked your way to the end of the taking water.

Salmon aren't very spooky in rivers. They seem oblivious to the bank-side tremors, overhead shadows, and wading fishermen (up to a point) that give trout conniptions. You can even throw rocks at salmon and they won't go away—in fact, sometimes this seems to stir them up to the point where they'll take a fly they've refused time and again. But given the salmon's general indifference to its surroundings, it's amazing how swiftly and aggressively the fish will react to a fly that either invades its immediate "space" or invades that space in a way the fish suddenly finds interesting.

The Atlantic salmon is an itinerant fish pursued by anglers as it undergoes a biological change that affects its most basic behavior—feeding. This dictates an entirely different approach from that of most other types of fishing, in which fish are gulled with food or imitations thereof.

The salmon angler must think *big*—macro- rather than micro-environments. He must consider weather events, such as drenching rains that raise rivers and bring in or move fish. Trout seek cozy, isolated little pockets providing food, comfort, and protection, but salmon lies are formed by the interaction of powerful aquatic forces (water height and flow speed) with static riverbed structures, creating resting places where traveling salmon feel comfortable. These lies can't always be identified by just looking at the surface of the water or the riverbank, although current speed and visible structure will suggest their existence.

There's an old saw that the three most important factors in real estate are location, location, and location. This is also true of salmon fishing. The second great pillar upon which successful salmon fishing rests is: *Learn to identify the resting lies of salmon.* Salmon are most vulnerable to a fly when they're resting during their journey upstream, and they seek two kinds of rest: long-term, which they find in deep holding pools, and short-term, which they find in areas of comfort that they rarely inhabit for more than a day or two.

Even great rivers contain only a handful of holding pools. These are easily identified and heavily fished. Many successful anglers spend much of their time on secondary pools or in runs where salmon rest for relatively brief periods, in short-term lies created by specific water conditions.

Identifying good resting habitat or lies is as important to the salmon fisher as insect identification is to the trout angler. The specific requirements of a resting lie are best understood by harking back to the childhood game of flying your hand out the car window. Angle your hand slightly upward and the wind snatches your arm up; angle it slightly downward and the wind quickly pushes your arm down. But if you hold your hand so it just attains a state of equilibrium, the wind has no effect at all; the car might as well be parked.

In a resting lie, salmon seek relief from their upstream battle against the current. They also want a peculiar form of comfort and security that they seem only to find in relatively open water. Unlike trout, or even their anadromous relative the steelhead, Atlantic salmon generally don't like bankside lies, "holes," or resting lies under large deadfalls or other riparian structures.

A good resting lie is usually in an open area where a brisk current, a depth of at least 3 feet, and sufficient bottom structure combine to create a place where the salmon can attain a nearly perfect state of equilibrium. In that state a salmon can simultaneously maintain its position against the current and extract sufficient oxygen from the water washing over its gills—without making an effort to do either. A lie can offer such a desirable combination of these features that a succession of salmon will rest in precisely the same location (say, 2 feet below a flat gray rock and in the depression just before a yellow one) day after day, year after year!

Although salmon fishing is almost always discussed in terms of "pools," many of the very best salmon pools are more accurately described as runs. Even in a conspicuous pool—the kind of place where a kid would hang a tire from an overhanging tree—salmon are likely to be found in its run, where the swift water enters, or down near its glassy tail, where the water begins to pick up speed again.

Learn to identify good resting or holding lies and you will be fishing over salmon—or at least you'll be doing so if salmon are present. This brings us to the last pillar: *Find out if salmon are present where you intend to fish, and if they aren't, go looking for them.*

A good deal of salmon fishing could be more accurately described as salmon hunting. This is an agreeable enterprise—climbing trees, peering off bridges, bushwhacking—that can alleviate the tedium of the classic step-cast-step wet-fly method. Yes, sometimes high or turbid water demands that you fish "blind," but you needn't always fish that way.

These, then, are the three most important things an aspiring salmon angler must learn to do: understand the nature of the fish, read the water to find resting places, and find salmon. The rest is mere technique, and the good news for novices is that technique—at least in the sense that it implies formidable skills in casting or fly manipulation—usually doesn't play a decisive role in successful salmon fishing. Neither does fly selection.

My friend Jim Emery once took a veteran trout fisherman on a salmon fishing trip. The angler had done some homework and came armed with a nice assortment of salmon flies. Jim put him in a good pool on the Matapedia, near a big underwater rock at the head of a long, productive run. Jim wished him luck and disappeared around the bend.

When Jim returned a few hours later, he was pleasantly surprised to see the man back at the head of the pool, apparently ready to pass through again with a different fly in the usual step-cast-step drill. After all, patience is not merely a virtue in salmon fishing, it's an element of character without which veterans will never take you seriously, no matter how much you know.

"How many times through?" Jim called out, standing on the high bank.

"None," the man replied. "I've been working this rock."

As it turned out, despite all the man had read and all the advice Jim had given him on the long drive up, he could not—or would not—let go of the conviction that if he passed enough flies by the big rock he might eventually come up with one that would trigger a take.

From the high bank under the midday sun, Jim could see there was no salmon—no nothing—anywhere within 20 feet of the rock.

Remember: location, location, location. Look, look, look.

CHAPTER 2

Salmon Country

Some years ago, my friend Isabelle Fritz-Cope accompanied me on a two-week auto tour of Canada's salmon country. She wanted to fish for salmon, she was curious about the remote Gaspe Peninsula, and she was eager to practice her considerable command of the French language with the Quebecois.

After spending three pleasant days at Tucker Cluett's camp on the Upsalquitch in New Brunswick, we left for Quebec and the Bonaventure, a gem of a Gaspe river that flows south out of the Chic-Chocs Mountains into the Bay of Chaleur. About four hours into the drive we pulled off scenic Route 132, which hugs the coast along the entire peninsula and passes through dozens of quaint, neat fishing villages along the way. We planned a roadside lunch of fresh, steamed lobster bought for a dollar a pound from a roadside *poissonerie,* and stopped at a convenience store— a *dépanneur*—to buy some wine and incidentals.

Isabelle greeted the owner and in perfect French politely told him our needs. As he answered, Isabelle's jaw dropped in small increments that expressed her utter incomprehension. She learned firsthand that

Gaspe French is so far removed from the mother tongue that it may as well be Cantonese.

Such unexpected features of provincial life may be inconvenient, but they also add to the charm and sense of adventure an angler feels in North America's salmon country. Popular trout fishing destinations in the United States, including the great rivers of our western states, are not only crowded with fishermen but also awash in nouveau fly-fishing culture. Towns on many rivers today have more tackle shops than gas stations or hardware stores. Garish neon reflections now dance on the Madison's riffles near the old South Fork campsite, because some enterprising soul decided fly fishers needed a bankside tavern in which to congregate after a day's fishing.

Salmon country is different. There are places on the Gaspe where replacing a broken rod or reel means driving two or three hours to a "tackle shop" in the basement of a private home—whose owner may be away on a two-week visit to his in-laws. There are public fishing beats in salmon country where losing a set of car keys means a 10-mile walk out—not to a car dealership, but to a road with enough traffic to hitch a 10-mile ride to the nearest telephone.

You don't want to arrive on a branch of the upper Petite Cascapedia only to realize that you left your bug dope back in the motel, and you certainly want to have a backup fly line handy in case you did remember the bug dope but accidentally spilled it on your line and melted off the plastic coating.

The Gaspe is beautiful and frequently spectacular, a remarkably satisfying but underutilized tourist destination. It offers relatively few tourist amenities beyond the excellent ones found in the coastal towns, some of which enjoy a brief but busy summer beach season. But as soon as you head inland on the Gaspe—and by inland I mean as little as ¼ mile from the water's edge—service establishments and even habitations quickly vanish, often giving way to forests of aspen and pine so thick you can barely peer into them.

Before I describe the boundaries of salmon country and the variety of fishing opportunities available in it, let me return briefly to that first day Isabelle and I spent on the Gaspe. I included the Bonaventure River in our itinerary because, while it's almost entirely a public river, it's renowned for

The River Bonaventure (Photo: Richard Franklin)

its water clarity, and for the beauty and solitude of its wild upper river valley. Other than that, I knew next to nothing about the Bonaventure.

A few hours after our lobster lunch, we arrived at the town of Bonaventure. We took the only road heading north at the main inter-section in town and soon came to a bridge over the river. There were fishermen in the long, appealing pool below the bridge, and we decided to stop and watch them and give Isabelle's beagle, Lexington, a little exercise. As soon as we let Lexi out of the jeep, she bolted down the gravel beach. I didn't think much of it until I noticed the loaded picnic table 200 yards away.

I began to sprint down the beach, screaming Lexi's name. Ignoring me, she hopped up on the table and began to root through the comestibles. To make matters worse, one of the anglers was just coming back off the river. He reached the table a moment before I did, while Lexi—feeling pressured from all sides now—inhaled the last bit of a ham sandwich.

Apologizing profusely, I offered to drive back to town to get the man another sandwich. He laughed, assuring me that he had more food in the cooler. His name was Glen LeGrand, and he was guiding the

American anglers fishing near the bridge. We got to talking, and Glen gave me a quick education in the river. Thanks to his advice, we were able to fish confidently, in the best available water, from the get-go.

That kind of felicitous encounter is also part of the Gaspe experience.

Incidentally, Glen grew up near the Bonaventure, but he could not legally fish there as a youth because a few wealthy absentee owners controlled the entire river. Fortunately Glen's best boyhood friend not only shared his keen interest in fishing but also was the son of the head warden assigned to protect the river while its owners were away. The two boys, armed with insider's knowledge of the warden's daily whereabouts, became expert poachers. After the river went public, Glen did so well as a guide that by 1995 he was able to build and open a magnificent commercial lodge located right on the banks of the lower river: Camp Bonaventure.

Aspiring salmon anglers from the United States are sometimes put off by the Byzantine regulations that govern most Canadian salmon fishing. They're accustomed to buying resident or visitor licenses and going fishing, period. The greatest restriction they're apt to encounter is a property owner who won't allow fishermen to cross his meadow to get to the river. Although salmon fishing in the United States and the province of Nova Scotia is a straightforward enterprise, getting access to salmon water in other provinces can be considerably more complicated and expensive. Appendix I provides a province-by-province guide to public fishing regulations and opportunities. In this chapter we'll just take a quick tour of salmon country, and I'll identify and comment on the various systems in use.

MAINE

Salmon country in North America begins near Bangor, Maine. All the salmon fishing in the United States is public, but what little there is takes place mostly on Maine's Penobscot River. Other salmon rivers, such as the Machias and Narraguagus, are small and barely able to sustain fishable salmon populations. The Penobscot is a wide (about 150 yards), relatively shallow river with only a few miles of fishable water, most of it running right through the Bangor city limits. The fishery ends abruptly at Veazie Dam.

The indigenous Penobscot strain of salmon was wiped out long ago, and today's fish are genetic descendants of various Canadian salmon from which hatchery technicians have tried to create a new resident fish. A dearth of spawning habitat and environmental degradation of various kinds above Veazie make the Penobscot a hatchery-dependent system. A fish trap at the base of the dam enables hatchery personnel to remove fish from the river, after which they're trucked to a nearby hatchery. There the fish are stripped of milt and eggs, and their progeny are raised to the *smolt* stage (the phase at which young salmon go to sea) at the hatchery before they are released into the river to face their daunting journey to the high seas.

The Penobscot salmon stack up in the pools, runs, and channels of the broad, flat river below the dam. During peak season, before the tea-colored water becomes so warm that the fish turn dour, the Penobscot is productive. Because of the dam, the fish are a captive audience to anglers' flies. But the river is rarely easy, partly because of the number of anglers fishing in Rotation (see chapter 11 for more on this) through every pool. Penobscot salmon see an endless array of flies and soon become inured to them. The Penobscot experience isn't at all representative of salmon fishing in general, but it's all there really is in the United States.

Anglers for salmon in Maine must purchase a "salmon stamp" in addition to their resident or nonresident licenses.

NOVA SCOTIA

Nova Scotia offers varied, premium fishing opportunities as well as universal public fishing. This English-speaking province is pastoral and picturesque. Its coastline is steeped in commercial fishing lore and tradition—but it also has some wonderful rivers that produce good runs of wild salmon. You can fish any Nova Scotian salmon river you like, as much as you like, for the price of your fishing license. Access generally isn't a problem in this friendly part of the world.

Conservationists concerned with stress on the resource sometimes criticize this "open" policy, as do local anglers, who resent the annual invasion of Nova Scotia's fine, fall-run rivers by American fishermen, many of them senior citizens who park their recreational vehicles beside salmon rivers and fish for weeks at a time.

While a simple license entitles you to fish every day of the salmon season in Nova Scotia, the tag system (see appendix I) and catch-and-release-only regulations for MSW fish limit the salmon you may kill to a number comparable with provinces where daily fishing rights are more restricted. If you choose to keep fish and use up your maximum seasonal quota of eight tags in a hot week of fishing in early June, you're finished for the year.

Nova Scotia is a great bargain, and there's something that feels right about not having to pay a daily fishing fee on top of the cost of your license. There's much less pressure to make the most of your pay-by-the-day fishing and more latitude on how much you fish as well as when and where you do so. Given the importance of unpredictable factors such as weather, water conditions, and the timing of the run, this can be a great advantage. The best things about the system are that you can hopscotch around to different rivers in the same day, and that you don't have to deal with the costly and inconvenient logistics of purchasing or renewing your day ticket.

Unfortunately, in recent years many of Nova Scotia's summer-run rivers have been blighted by a host of environmental problems, ranging from lethal acidification to excessive siltation to unacceptably high water temperatures due to chronic summer drought conditions. But the province still offers some spectacular fall fishing on small *spate* rivers (those dependent on rainfall rather than springs or a natural or man-made reservoir) as well as the renowned Margaree on Cape Breton Island.

A word about fall-run salmon: On most Canadian salmon rivers, some fish don't even enter until long after the main summer run has passed through. Some rivers even have minor late-summer or early-fall runs of fish that appear to be a unique strain of the river's summer-run fish. On the Upsalquitch and some other rivers, these fish are called bluebacks (for the obvious reason). These late-run salmon are another example of the overlap nature has developed as an insurance policy against the dangers of having all fish on the same schedule.

But some rivers have full-blown fall runs of salmon that are clearly an entirely different strain of fish, rather than merely a generational segment of summer-run fish biologically programmed to enter a river late. Certain rivers in New Brunswick and Nova Scotia—provinces more apt to suffer from low and excessively warm water during the summer—have major runs of fall fish. This suggests that in those places, a true strain of fall-run fish developed over the centuries in response to environmental conditions. On the Margaree, those fish ultimately came to enjoy such a survival advantage over summer-run fish that as time—and the human impact on rivers—progressed, the fall run has become larger and more important.

At any rate, fall fishing can be great fun during this most spectacular and invigorating time of year. It can also be a difficult, daunting challenge that only veteran salmon fishers ought to undertake; high water levels, wind, unseasonably cold weather, and low water temperatures may dictate the use of special equipment and techniques that I'm unable to cover satisfactorily in this book.

NEW BRUNSWICK

The province of New Brunswick takes a radically different and vastly more complicated approach to salmon management and fishing. Coastal New Brunswick is relatively populous, with good farmland, significant light industry, and broad, pleasant river valleys. The province maintains the traditional practice of leasing out salmon water, and it raises significant revenue from selling those leases at auction to camp operators who maintain commercial or private camps.

The province also pioneered the progressive catch-and-release-only policy for MSW salmon that is now common in salmon country, and the fishing has dramatically improved provincewide because of it.

New Brunswick salmon fishing represents a remarkable patchwork quilt of leased, private, and public water that can be nearly impossible to figure out, but that ultimately proves the province recognizes recreational fishing as a powerful revenue-generating industry.

In New Brunswick *all* nonresidents must fish with provincially certified guides. As a result most visitors fish out of commercial camps that own or lease water and provide guides. Generally the cost of a one-week salmon fishing vacation at these camps is reasonable (about $1,500

Canadian). You can also hire a local guide (for about $150 per day) and leave the procurement of water up to him, but an inexperienced salmon fisher should only do so with guidance from a veteran.

The angler accustomed to the guides who work on many of the premium North American trout rivers may not be ready to appreciate the "typical" Canadian salmon guide. Generally he's a reserved man with conservative values, one of which is that even if you do know a great deal, you don't go around broadcasting it. Often he's suspicious of—or indifferent to—the unfamiliar. Don't expect him to have much of an opinion on the latest rage in synthetic fly-tying or rod-building materials. Don't expect him to make an impassioned speech in the stern of the canoe denouncing the Japanese high-seas fishing fleet for its poaching of Pacific salmon. Don't wonder if he has a "real" story, like so many of the American guides, who can talk of professional burnout, substance abuse, broken marriages, and the decision to leave all that behind and become a guide.

No, the classic Canadian guide is first and foremost a riverman, almost always born on or near the water to a family with a rich fishing and guiding tradition. Most of the time he won't even be an "expert" salmon fisherman, familiar with such techniques as the greased-line fishing method. But he will have a great grasp of what works on the river where *he* works, and, most significant, he will almost always know that river and its features the way you know your living room and its furniture.

Fish with him long enough (you measure it in years, not days) and he may decide that you're okay even though you talk a Godawful lot and have crazy theories about Flashabou and smolt stocking in Norway (where you've never been).

Fish with him long enough and you may decide that he's okay, too, because he sees fish long before you do, he knows a great deal about the river and the country around it that he tells you in tiny installments, and he gets you fish without ever making a big fuss about it.

There is the occasional crook, blowhard, or drunkard among Canadian guides (I've shared a whiskey with a number of them), which is why it really pays to hire one who comes recommended by other anglers or reliable local sources, such as conservation agencies.

Salmon fishing in most of New Brunswick is like a folk art, embedded deeply in the culture and accessible to all. The province is a cozy, comfortable place to fish. Anglers in thrall to the aura of salmon fishing would be surprised by the homespun ambience that characterizes the most productive salmon watershed in North America, the vast Miramichi River system. That watershed is a maze of small private and commercial camps, leased pools, privately owned pools, and Mom-and-Pop guiding operations. People overlap, share, help each other out. The fishing and the culture are integrated.

QUEBEC

This pastoral picture changes as you head north toward the border with Quebec and the Bay of Chaleur. Gradually the mill towns and farm communities give way to vast stretches of moose bogs and timber, plateaus and rolling hills dedicated to the only major industry that still matters this far north—logging. Now and then you cross a salmon river, but ultimately you arrive at the epicenter of salmon country, the estuary just below the small town of Matapedia, Quebec, where the Restigouche and Matapedia Rivers converge to create the Bay of Chaleur. The nearest town of any size is Campbellton, New Brunswick.

The steel bridge at Matapedia is the border between the provinces of New Brunswick and Quebec; just above it, the Restigouche flows in from New Brunswick to meet the Matapedia, which is entirely in Quebec. The differences between these sister rivers—both of which are famous for their large salmon—and the way they are managed make a powerful statement about provincial history, politics, and conservation.

Although the lower Restigouche marks the provincial boundary between New Brunswick and Quebec, it is essentially a New Brunswick river. With the exception of a few pools in its tidewater, the Restigouche and a great deal of the water on its main tributaries (including the Upsalquitch and Kedgwick, both New Brunswick rivers) is privately held under the lease system, mostly by wealthy individuals or organizations such as the exclusive Restigouche Salmon Club. The commercial camps on the river charge up to $7,000 Canadian for a week of fishing, and get plenty of takers at that price.

While conservative New Brunswick has maintained the tradition of leasing water to the highest bidder, showing no particular prejudice

One of the historic salmon lodges along New Brunswick's famed Restigouche River (Photo: Val Atkinson)

toward foreign lessors, the face of salmon fishing in Quebec was drastically altered by the popular, militant agenda of the Francophone independence movement. In the late 1960s, the Quebecois launched a purge of private control of the salmon fishery throughout the province and aggressively instituted a policy geared toward creating more public fishing opportunities. The Matapedia and most of the other Gaspe rivers were radically transformed.

Today the Matapedia has very little private water and only two significant commercial camps, Cold Spring and Tobique. The management system offers two levels of public fishing: water reserved for lucky anglers during an annual lottery (see appendix I) on the historic and highly productive Glen Emma section, and day-ticket, open-to-all-comers fishing on the upper river.

The fishing on the Glen Emma compares to the best fishing offered at any private camp anywhere in Canada. For about $450 Canadian per day you get guided fishing from a canoe on your very own private beat of prime pools, all of which are likely to hold numbers of fish during prime time.

Inside a salmon camp on the Gaspe Peninsula of Quebec (Photo: Val Atkinson)

The upper day-ticket water also has many fine pools, including the storied Salmon Hole and the Forks Pool, where the Causapscal tributary joins the Matapedia. The fishing on the upper river is available to any licensed resident or visitor, on any day, for the price of a license and a day ticket—about $65 Canadian, or roughly $50 U.S. (see appendix I). It can be relatively crowded and competitive, and the fishing can be very challenging because of it. But the fish are always there. On any given day you'll cast a fly over visible, 30-pound fish.

Although the system in Quebec is undoubtedly more "democratic," the province has not followed New Brunswick's enlightened conservation policy. Quebec has a complicated bag limit that often allows the angler to keep an MSW salmon as well as a grilse, and the peculiarities of the order in which they are caught and killed creates opportunities for abuse.

While the Restigouche and its New Brunswick tributaries flow mostly through rugged country with limited road access to much of the watershed, the Matapedia is accessible from any direction by good highways. Route 132, the major north–south artery at the base of the Gaspe, runs along the entire length of the river.

Anglers fishing the famed Salmon Hole can regularly feel the ground tremble as 18-wheelers roar by on the highway carved into the steep bank above the river. The Matapedia attracts many sports from the New York metropolitan area. They can leave New York City at dawn and arrive in Causapscal that evening in time to purchase their nonresident licenses and next-day fishing permits. A nonresident season license costs about $75 U.S.

There are a number of motels along the river, some rental cabins, a few campgrounds, grocery stores (many of which also stock salmon flies), and even a small 24-hour truckers' restaurant where fishermen and freight haulers sometimes share tables in the wee hours before daybreak. The Matapedia is a user-friendly river for public-water anglers, but it lacks the solitude and unspoiled natural beauty offered by many other Quebec rivers.

The south shore of the Gaspe Peninsula begins at the Matapedia-Restigouche estuary and forms the northern boundary of the Bay of Chaleur. As you follow the southern coast of the Gaspe eastward on Route 132, you drive through a succession of resort villages distinguished by tidy, colorful homes featuring lavish flower boxes and the gleaming, tin-faced spires of the churches that often dominate the towns. This road is called the Salmon Highway and it eventually leads clear round the Gaspe and back westward along the north shore of the peninsula (the South Shore of the Gulf of Saint Lawrence).

This is a great three-day trip for any tourist. But for the salmon fisherman it's also a grand tour of the greatest concentration of outstanding salmon rivers in the world. Just a few hours east of the Matapedia you cross the Grand Cascapedia, then the Petite Cascapedia. Next come the Bonaventure, the Ste. Jean, and the York.

On the Gaspe, many of the rivers are managed by the *ZEC system*. This acronym stands for *Zone d'Exploitation Contrôlée,* which translates to "controlled exploitation zone." The ZECs are interesting grassroots cooperatives composed of local anglers who manage the fishing on the river, fulfilling the same role that the official provincial facilities do on rivers such as the Matapedia. The ZECs issue all fishing permits, licenses, river maps, and general information in offices that are usually located right on the rivers. These offices are great focal points for anglers and good places to get up-to-date information on everything from river conditions throughout the Gaspe to fly preferences on the local river.

As you round the blunt tip of the peninsula near the town of Gaspe and begin to head back, you cross the Dartmouth, then the Madelaine, the Ste. Anne, and the Cap Chat. Along the way are some small, lesser-known rivers that still have modest runs of fish, and rivers that once supported salmon but from which the fish has been eradicated. It goes on like that, with a deeply satisfying cadence, until you come almost full circle and find yourself near the headwaters of the Matapedia near a town called Matane, for the river that flows through it.

The Matane is one of my favorite public fisheries in Canada. The fish in this clear, relatively small river tend to arrive later, offering good sport in August and September, and the entire river is open to the public on a day-ticket basis. The things I most like about the Matane are its spectacular scenery and its variety of pools. There are far fewer amenities along the Matane than the Matapedia, and many miles of its fine upper water are accessible only via a dirt road that follows the narrow, fetching river valley. The driving time to the Matane from most Canadian and U.S. destinations is about the same as it is for the Matapedia.

The fishway in the dam at the town of Matane, where the river flows into the Saint Lawrence, is open to the public. It has a viewing window where salmon can be seen under water, ascending the ladder. It also has a fish counter, so it's easy to know when the main run of fish has arrived and entered the river.

There's a wonderful symmetry to this trip via Route 132 around the Gaspe. If you start eastward from the town of Matapedia you can make a left just about anywhere along the way, and in what seems like the blink of an eye leave behind the stony beaches and the hard blue ocean of the coast and find yourself up in the cool, fragrant deep woods, on a winding road along a swift, clear, muscular salmon river.

Of course there's a lot more Canadian salmon fishing beyond the Gaspe. There's the majestic North Shore, the east coast of Quebec on the northwest edge of the Saint Lawrence. The North Shore also has many fine salmon rivers, including the mighty—and mighty exclusive—Moisie.

Then there's Newfoundland and Labrador, both of which offer widespread public salmon fishing opportunities.

But now we're getting into increasingly remote areas, where just knocking around salmon fishing demands a serious commitment of time and some careful planning, or where the fishing is best experienced for the first time with the help of an outfitter and camp operator. The great thing about salmon country is that it simultaneously offers variety and—because of the specific requirements of salmon—a charming and comforting similarity.

CHAPTER 3

When to Go

The ancient cliché suggests that the best time to go fishing is anytime you can get away. This is patently untrue of salmon fishing.

The best time to go salmon fishing is after a hard rain, when a river, no longer influenced by snow runoff or the annual spring freshet, undergoes a significant *rise* of water (6 inches or more). Although fishing can be good on the rising water, the best fishing occurs when the river begins to clear and subside; at that time the differences between pools and runs again become pronounced. A significant rise of water often brings in fresh fish from the estuary, and it *always* gets the fish that are already in the river moving upstream.

How much time passes between dead high water and the optimal fishing level depends on the amount of rainfall and the nature of the river. Rivers on the barren, rocky coast of Scotland can go from trickles to torrents and back to trickles in a day or two. The same volume of water falling on the forested, water-absorbent mountains of Quebec can keep a river in transition for a week or longer. In Canada, heavy rain at the start of your weeklong fishing trip can wash out the sport for two days but still provide you with great fishing the rest of the week.

This universal truth about salmon fishing illustrates the extent to which variable and unpredictable river conditions dramatically influence the sport, more so than in most other types of angling. It's an open secret that, under perfect conditions on a good river, salmon fishing with a wet fly can be child's play. In fact, a dedicated brown trout fisherman once told me that he enjoyed such ideal conditions on his first-ever salmon trip that he never went again because the fishing was "too easy."

But under difficult water conditions, the most experienced and attentive angler can fish for days with the most sophisticated of techniques and the utmost dedication and still end up skunked. I consider this one of the great charms of salmon fishing: Nature, and not the angler and his expertise, retains ultimate command. It also vividly demonstrates the complicated interdependence of all the components making up the organic world of the salmon.

The basic unpredictability of the sport helps define the salmon fisher as something of a gambler. A home-run hitter. An individual willing to take risks and endure frustrations commensurate with the quality of the reward. Salmon fishers have always lived by the jazzy bodybuilders' slogan: "No pain, no gain."

The two most important factors in evaluating river conditions are *water level* (height) and *temperature.* Of these, level is more important, partly because it's also a determining factor in water temperature. Water level can powerfully impact every aspect of your experience, including the type of equipment you use, the size and style of the flies you fish, and whether you fish from a canoe or wade. More important, water level and temperature can also determine the number and mood of the fish in the river, as well as the suitability of the pools for salmon and the ways you fish those pools.

WATER LEVEL

Salmon prefer to enter a river on high water, and they'll travel upriver as briskly as conditions and their individual determinants allow. The steady, cold torrent of the early season, as well as high water once the season is well under way, encourages fish to keep moving. These traveling fish pause here and there to rest, and in these temporary or transitional lies they're often vulnerable to a fly. In fact, such fish seem particularly aggressive. Once water levels begin to recede, fish that aren't hell-bent on reaching the headwaters before the fiddleheads unfurl stop more often, in more predictable places, and for longer periods.

Water conditions heavily influence a salmon's behavior as well as the rate and time at which it travels. Under normal to low water levels, salmon prefer to travel at night, especially on rivers where they must negotiate shallow gravel bars or riffles along the way. They spend the better part of the daylight hours settled into comfortable lies in pools or runs. The fish seem to follow this pattern most predictably on falling water, when the abundance of water keeps them moving but the variety of conditions they encounter—particularly long, shallow riffles or stretches of whitewater—leads them to stop in comfortable locations.

Generally a salmon responds best to a fly in the morning, shortly after moving into a new resting lie in a pool, or in the evening, as it prepares to leave a lie and continue upstream. At those optimal angling times, the fish can appear as cranky as a tired human traveler or as nervous as a first-time airline passenger. It may chase and slash at flies without taking them, roll on the surface, or *flash*—list quickly to one side, exposing a broad silver flank that can appear to the astonished angler as an enormous sheet of submerged aluminum foil momentarily catching the sunlight.

As "normal" water continues to drop because of a lack of rainfall, salmon become more likely to wait in pools until a rise of water triggers their urge to move again. During prolonged dry periods, the fish lose their urgency to travel. They grow lethargic and become less likely to take a fly. At this time many fish settle into major holding pools, where some linger for weeks in the same lie, waiting for a change in the weather before attempting the next leg of their journey.

Usually these *stale* fish show no reaction whatsoever to a fly. They may even appear catatonic. But suddenly one may bolt forward, lap the pool, leap high into the air, then return to exactly the same position it previously occupied. If you can see this and refrain from breaking your rod over your knee and marching back to camp, you may be a salmon fisher after all.

Water level has an impact on the viability of potential pools and lies. No matter how many pools a salmon river has, the majority fish best under specific conditions ranging from high to low water. (Throughout this book, unless otherwise indicated, I assume that water conditions are "normal," or moderate.) The rules of thumb are: *High-water pools need strong flows and above-average water levels to hold fish;* and, *Low-water pools need moderate flows and lower water levels to offer the fish good resting lies.*

Individual lies are strongly influenced by water level. Remember, a good lie is created by the ideal combination of depth, current speed, and bottom structure. High water always creates greater depth and faster current, while low water reduces depth and current speed.

High water is also much more difficult to interpret than low water, partly because there's so much of it, and it's impossible for the above-water angler to interpret the degree of turbulence and current conflict below the surface. Basically, the challenge of high-water fishing is finding resting salmon; the problems posed by low water have more to do with the fish's receptivity.

TEMPERATURE

Water temperature is related to water level but not strictly controlled by it—at least not on a healthy river. In 1995 I fished the Ste. Jean River on the Gaspe under severe drought and heat wave conditions. Yet the water temperature on the upper river was about 62 degrees Fahrenheit in the morning and never quite hit 70 in the afternoon. The Ste. Jean is a pristine, spring-fed river whose valley is so steep that it has never been logged; thus it has tremendous integrity of habitat. The thermal profiles of many larger rivers and their tributaries, including such outstanding ones as the Matapedia, Restigouche, Miramichi, and Grand Cascapedia, have been impacted more severely by development, logging, and road construction.

Salmon have been known to enter rivers on water temperatures as low as 34 degrees, but they rarely travel in frigid waters. Once the temperature rises to above 40 they move more readily, but they rarely take flies fished on or near the surface until the water hits 50 degrees. The best fishing occurs from that point on up to 68 degrees. Above 68, salmon grow lethargic, hole up in deeper, cooler pools, and become increasingly disinterested in flies. Grilse don't seem as sensitive to high water temperature as MSW salmon, however; I've had excellent grilse fishing in water in the low 70s.

The bottom end of the ideal temperature range is of little concern to most anglers, because such low temperatures rarely occur on Canadian rivers once the main run of fish enters fresh water. Although the entire 20-degree swing between 50 and 70 degrees can provide good fishing, I choose 62 as the magic number at which salmon are most inclined to take. Bear in mind that as the water temperature rises above 70, the stress of being caught may prove lethal for even the most artfully played and carefully released fish.

There are other homilies associated with water temperature, such as the popular beliefs that you should fish only with dry flies when the air is warmer than the water, or that the fishing is lousy when the combination of very warm air and cold water causes heavy mist to rise from the river. I've never found these generalizations reliable. By far the most important concern for most salmon anglers is excessively high water temperature; depending on the river and the weather, this can become a problem by early July.

Still, most anglers would prefer to gamble on the weather and fish in early to mid-July, because by then the main run of fish is almost always distributed throughout the river. That's the best reason to fish at this time—but it isn't the only one.

THE EARLY SEASON

In Atlantic Canada salmon season generally opens in early June, and under typical weather conditions in the lower portion of salmon country—New Brunswick and the rivers of the Gaspe Peninsula—the fishing usually peaks in early to mid-July. The peak period moves progressively later as you head north. MSW salmon invariably arrive first, and some of the mightiest fish usually lead the way.

I'm always amazed that when the season officially opens on the Matapedia, a good number of big (20- to 40-pound) salmon are already lined up with their noses pressed against the steel fence that halts their journey far up the river's Causapscal Branch. Clearly, salmon can ascend rivers of average length in just a few days, yet nature staggers the run and seems to imprint each individual fish with a timetable that we are hard put to predict or understand. But as a general rule the big spring fish lead the run, while the last fish are usually the grilse.

Another generalization that seems consistently true is that early-season salmon fishing is a feast-or-famine proposition. Chances are you'll catch nothing, but if you do get a fish it will be a big one.

I love to see a river running robustly, with the bankside trees freshly leafed out and the songbirds in full cry. I like all that available water in the early season, when a pool can have six or seven times more "taking water" than later in the summer. And I really like that there are fewer anglers on public water early in the season, particularly on the day-ticket beats. But although I've made a number of early-season trips, I've only hooked a few of those big early-season fish while wade fishing on public water.

The biggest problem with the early season has less to do with the relatively small number of fish than with the way they are programmed to take advantage of the ideal, round-the-clock traveling conditions offered by water that's cold enough to keep them vigorous and high enough to afford them comfort and security. And there's a downside to all that taking water: The fish have countless resting places available on their infrequent stops.

While I've come to believe that traveling fish are very vulnerable when they take up temporary, transitional resting lies, the odds against finding one are long. I've also come to enjoy pursuing visible salmon with a dry fly, and early in the season, on most rivers, that's nearly impossible.

Finally, wade fishing in cold, early-season water is always exhausting, particularly when using a one-handed rod (more about this later). A good salmon angler has the patience of Job, but he rarely has comparable physical stamina after three or four days spent up to his armpits in a cold river, meticulously combing one frigid 200-yard pool after another.

Nevertheless, spring fish have a definite aura and are undoubtedly among the strongest and wildest of salmon. The biggest I ever hooked, a fish in the 25-pound class, took my size 4 Brown Eel wet fly (a variation on the popular British tube fly, tied on a light-wire, extra-long-shank hook) in the heart of the deep Heppel Bridge Pool on the Matapedia. That was a classic early-season experience.

The salmon took the fly in water that's rarely productive during prime time, because the pool's depth, its slack current, and the bridge prevent the wading angler from covering the water effectively with the traditional down-and-across wet-fly presentation. An occasional fish is taken with a dry fly in that part of the pool during mid- to low-water conditions, but that's about it.

Early that season the pool was even deeper than usual. But there was enough flow through the gut to keep the fly moving, and I was using a two-handed rod with which I could make a good delivery and presentation. I chose the Brown Eel because the combination of its long, bear hair wing and light-wire hook allowed the fly to "float" nicely along, suspended even in slow water.

After a few days of fishing without so much as seeing a salmon, I was completely unprepared for the fierce, sudden strike that came in the "wrong" part of the pool. By the time I realized what was happening the fish had bolted downstream, turned, and headed back up. The spool of my British reel was overrunning, and I had a long downstream bag in my line. I reeled up and tightened on the fish, and it tore off across the river. I palmed the spool but put too much pressure on the unpredictable fish at the wrong time. The fly pulled out, opened by the salmon—and me— at the bend.

This fish must have moved up out of the pool's traditional hot spot, the tailout, seeking relief from the strong current, and was in deeper water than salmon usually prefer. It was probably lurking just a few feet below the surface, rather than in a traditional lie, in a state between activity and rest. That's why it was particularly susceptible to the fly's intrusion into its space, as evidenced by the ferocious strike.

The lessons: Spring fish can be (but aren't necessarily) found in unexpected places. The fishing itself is a high-stakes game, and you must be ready to take advantage of the few opportunities that come your way despite the tedium, fatigue, and discouragement bred by long periods of inaction. And with salmon fishing, where fishless days are more the rule than the exception, the corrosive effect of this should not be underestimated.

Although traveling fish found in temporary resting lies often won't move very far for a fly, they can be savage takers, epitomizing Falkus's aggression strike. By contrast, fish that settle into a lie in a pool more often exhibit the feeding habit response, deliberately following a fly across a pool before slowly and confidently engulfing it. In the early season even an experienced angler, as I was that time on the Matapedia, can be taken by surprise and made to feel like a bumbling fool.

These days I no longer try to cover vast amounts of water hoping to encounter fish. I prefer the old "head 'em off at the pass" approach that worked so well for the cowboys in old movies. This requires staking out and concentrating on a few strategic locations that offer either good, deep water (typical holding pools) or good temporary resting lies in a relatively small, easily defined area, such as the tailout of a pool just above heavy whitewater, or water slow enough to afford fish rest just below a *choke,* where a great volume of water passes through a narrow channel.

The one thing I have learned is that you've got a much better chance of intercepting *anything* if you stand still rather than run around hoping to bump into it.

PRIME TIME

The main run of salmon often takes place soon after the first wave of large spring fish moves through the river on high water. By mid-June the water is often at the ideal height to create the desired definition of pools, runs, and riffles. These different types of water cause the salmon to adopt a travel-rest-travel itinerary, and rising but still comfortable water temperatures may also dampen their urgency to get upstream. This is *prime time,* and one way to identify it is by trying to book time at a camp. If there's no room at the inn, it's peak season.

Even on rivers with strong grilse runs, the precocious salmon are rarely mixed in with the main body of MSW fish. One day—usually around July 4 in New Brunswick—the grilse suddenly arrive in an identifiable third wave. The ratio of grilse to salmon varies tremendously from river to river, due to genetic factors and, to a certain extent, human tampering. (For instance, commercial fishermen target MSW fish by using gillnets with a larger mesh size, meaning that more grilse escape.)

The Upsalquitch River (Photo: Richard Franklin)

Some river systems are known as almost exclusively MSW rivers, while others feature small runs of salmon and droves of grilse.

On rivers with small grilse runs, it's a toss-up whether a hooked fish is a salmon or a grilse at any point during the season. But on rivers with large grilse runs (some of the great rivers of Newfoundland and some Miramichi tributaries have become almost exclusively grilse rivers), the odds of hooking an MSW salmon by the middle of July may be as low as 1 in 20. Provincial conservation agencies count MSW salmon and grilse separately, so it's easy enough to find out the ratio of salmon to grilse on any given river.

The Restigouche is principally an MSW salmon river. Yet its tributary, the Upsalquitch, gets a strong, distinct run of grilse that eventually outnumber the MSW salmon. These Upsalquitch grilse travel through the lower Restiguouche, then collectively turn left into the Upsalquitch. Now the Kedgwick, a tributary much farther up the Restigouche, gets MSW fish almost exclusively—including some of the largest salmon in the entire river system.

This apparent whim of nature may have developed because of the character of these rivers. Although the Kedgwick is smaller than the Upsalquitch, it's swift, deep, and well protected by riparian trees and brush. The lower reaches of the Upsalquitch are gentler, broader, and much more prone to spread; this not only raises water temperature but also creates shallow flats and riffles that make upstream passage for MSW fish more arduous and potentially hazardous. For these reasons nature may have built into the Upsalquitch strain a larger percentage of grilse. Predators such as bears, Native Canadians, and colonists also may have affected the salmon-to-grilse ratio over time.

One thing seems certain: The gillnetters who traditionally set up in the Restigouche estuary had the same chance of taking main river and tributary fish, so the difference in the upstream, stream-by-stream salmon-to-grilse ratios can't be attributed to discriminatory overfishing in the salt.

Given the impetuosity of grilse, rivers that have good runs of large ones (the grilse on the Upsalquitch can weigh up to 4 pounds plus) can offer spectacular action once the fish arrive. And on top-quality rivers with large runs of fish, some fresh MSW salmon are always mixed in with the grilse.

LATE SEASON

Come late July and August, most of the annual run is in the river. Many of the fish are already up in the cool headwaters, where they are often protected by law against fishing. There may be very few fish in the lower reaches of any given river at this time (the exceptions are rivers with late runs, such as the Matane), but the farther upriver you go, the more chance you have of finding salmon.

Under normal climatic conditions these are the *dog days,* with the lethargy induced by warm water compounding the salmon's increasing indifference to flies. The biological changes related to spawning are now visible. As the fish lose their bright color and take on coppery hues, those remaining in the main river often settle into upstream holding pools, conserving fat reserves for the rigors of spawning. All this translates into extremely difficult fishing.

On the other hand there are two encouraging facets of late-season angling: The river has plenty of fish, and many of them may be visible. In addition the salmon not only take dry flies at this time of year but often prefer them to wet flies. Still, even though these conditions define the type of fishing I most enjoy, they don't really offset the general list-lessness I feel during the dog days. I also lose my taste for fishing when I see a river in its weakest, unhappiest state.

Fortunately some of the downside is eliminated on rivers that continue to maintain acceptable water temperatures through the dog days, and on the few rivers that have "late"—as opposed to fall—runs. (Most of those are cold rivers, which is probably how they evolved into late-run rivers.) Cold water seems to retard metabolic changes, such as the loss of weight and bright color, so late-run fish remain "fresh" that much longer.

Unseasonably cool and wet weather in July and August can also create good fishing on rivers that usually suffer during those months. Although I haven't experienced it, I'm told that surprisingly good fishing can be had in August when a stressed river is revitalized by a cool spell or a significant rise of water after a heavy rainfall. On popular rivers such as the Miramichi and Matapedia, the prime-time anglers are usually gone by the second week of August, which means the enterprising or lucky late-season angler who happens to be on the river during a positive change of conditions will enjoy quality fishing without the crowding or loss of privacy of peak season.

It really isn't worth gambling on this possibility when planning a trip in advance, but it's a good thing to keep in mind if you can get away for a short trip on a moment's notice—particularly if you're fishing on a more viable cold-water fishery in August where the action is slow. It's surprising how many people aren't sufficiently flexible to change plans when conditions change. But this underscores a basic commandment that salmon anglers should always keep in mind: Once the fish are in, good fishing is first and foremost a function of good water conditions.

CHAPTER 4

Gearing Up

One of the ironies of salmon fishing is that, while access or camp fees can be high, you don't really need a lot of expensive gear. Of course this doesn't stop gung-ho salmon anglers from going astream burdened like pack mules, their vests bulging with boxes and all manner of doodads and gizmos hanging off them like Christmas tree ornaments. Hey, you wouldn't want to be caught out on a river, 300 yards from the nearest road, without a combination knot tier, cigarette lighter, hook remover, and amyl nitrate dispenser, right?

After all, you have to tie on a fly to catch a fish, have a smoke to calm your nerves before you step into the river, remove the hook from your huge salmon, then revive your fishing buddy after he passes out at the sight of it.

On the other hand, if you're willing to spend five minutes sorting through your fly boxes you can go salmon fishing armed confidently only with one good-size box containing a mixture of wet and dry flies, two or three spools of tippet material, a thermometer, polarized glasses,

Typical salmon angling equipment (Photo: Val Atkinson)

a hemostat to pinch down hook barbs and remove hooks, and a bottle of bug dope.

When it comes to equipment, your polarized sunglasses are much more important than that lovingly machined reel you've admired in the catalogs. Although it never hurts to use a tapered leader, you can usually fish effectively for salmon with 9 feet of thin-diameter 12-pound-test monofilament. The way you fish your fly and where you fish it are much more important than the fly itself or the craftsmanship reflected in its construction. And because salmon flies are big, even if you leave your reading glasses back at camp, you'll probably still be able to tie on a fly on your first try.

With this in mind, let's get dressed up and rigged out for fishing.

THE WELL-DRESSED SALMON ANGLER

The weather in salmon country is often cool and, if you're really lucky, wet. The better the conditions for fishing, the more likely you'll wish you'd brought along warmer or drier clothing. Even during warm, dry periods the nighttime temperature on the Gaspe can dip into the 40s Fahrenheit. The mornings—a good time for fishing—are almost always nippy. Steep, narrow, heavily wooded valleys with cold rivers running through them become chilly just minutes after the sun sets, even on hot afternoons.

BOAT-FISHING GEAR

All this is much more important to the wading angler than to one who plans to fish mostly from a canoe or a boat. If you don't have much experience fishing from a boat, here are some basic tips to keep in mind. Unlike the wading angler, who is three-quarters waterproof because of his waders, the boat angler needs full-coverage rain gear (many camps and most individual guides provide this). I prefer an old-fashioned hooded poncho made of lightweight nylon. It provides adequate lap and leg protection and spares you the indignities of dancing your way into typical foul-weather pants while standing in a narrow canoe during a thunderstorm.

Guides working out of boats generally want their clients (particularly novice anglers) to stay in the boat throughout the angling, fighting, and landing process. When a fish is hooked from an anchored boat, the first thing a guide usually does is haul up the anchor and head for a clear area along the shore. The rest of the drama takes place with the angler standing in the boat at the shore and the guide waiting in the shallows just below the boat for the opportunity to net the fish. At a good camp with boats and expert guides, you can do all your fishing in jeans and deck shoes and never get your hands wet.

That has never been my style. The guides I fish with regularly on the Upsalquitch understand my desire to play a more active role in my own happiest moments, and I try to explain this to any new guide I engage. For those reasons, and because I hate to feel stranded anywhere, I always wear hip boots in a boat. In fact it's about the only real use I've found for hip boots (as opposed to chest-high waders), which guarantee that a wading angler will get wet.

I own only stocking-foot waders, because proper wading shoes offer superior support compared to boot-foot waders. Inexpensive rubber boot-foot hippers are ideal for boat fishing, but since I don't own a pair I often wear light wading shoes over my stocking-foot hip boots. This is partly for comfort, and partly because the metal studs that are such helpful additions to felt-sole wading boots are hell on the floorboards of a wooden boat. They can also destroy a brand-new fly line in no time if you step on the inevitable coils of line that accumulate in a boat.

I like to step out of the boat after I hook a fish and we pull into shore, and I have enough experience with both canoes and fish to do so without screwing up—most of the time. I like the teamwork that takes place when a guide and sport know and trust each other, and working in tandem also makes landing and releasing fish a smoother and quicker process. By the way, these are just some of the reasons for cultivating relationships with individual guides (and camps) rather than perpetually hunting for a better deal, better water, or a more expert guide.

In addition to full-coverage rain gear and hip boots, a good gear bag makes fishing from a boat more pleasurable. You can wear a fishing vest easily enough, but you'll be more comfortable without one. And if you decide to take off your vest, you'll find a canoe has few dry, handy places to put it. Besides, an angler in a boat doesn't need a wide array of easily accessible and secure pockets. A good water-resistant bag that you can just sling over your shoulder is a much better way to go.

WADE-FISHING GEAR

Wade fishing in salmon country, where the weather can fluctuate significantly in the course of 24 hours as well as over longer periods, requires more planning. The key to staying warm and dry is layering; good synthetic underlayers are a lighter, more compact, and less expensive way to stay comfortable than wearing bulky overlayers such as sweaters and jackets. The new polyester fleeces provide great warmth with almost no weight, and they wick away and dissipate moisture without retaining sweat—as does, say, a cotton T-shirt.

Fleece socks worn over a pair of medium-weight wool socks provide outstanding warmth and additional cushioning inside waders, and they dry very quickly. Synthetic long johns and tops are also versatile. I prefer the "military" or "polar" weights in these garments, because when it's chilly you're apt to feel uncomfortable much sooner if you're wearing not quite enough than if you're wearing a little too much. I'm particularly fond of long-sleeved tops that feature a zippered cowl neck.

The best of these new fishing garments are the fleece pants, essentially an improved version of common cotton sweats. They're warm, they're lightweight, and they perform the seemingly impossible: They make waders feel almost comfortable. And unlike cotton sweats, soaking-wet fleece pants hung on a branch in the sunlight dry virtually in front of your eyes.

Synthetic long johns and/or fleece pants worn under waders will cover any conditions you'll encounter during salmon season. As an added convenience, most of the fleece pants are cut full enough that you can wear them around camp or into grocery stores or restaurants without feeling too self-conscious.

I prefer lightweight nylon stocking-foot waders worn over appropriate underlayers. But if you're wade fishing before the middle of July, you may prefer neoprene waders. Neoprenes can become uncomfortably warm if you have to spend a lot of time out of the water on summer afternoons, especially if you have to do some walking. But salmon rivers in general are cold, and so are Canadian mornings.

If you're fishing public water, you may be astream at or around sunrise. If the weather is cool, the water is high, and you're covering a lot of water, you'll be happy to be wearing neoprenes—even at the height of a bright afternoon.

From mid-July on, you may find yourself wet wading in an old pair of shorts or donning neoprenes, depending on the weather conditions and the river you're fishing. For example, I fished on the storied Pavilion water on the Gaspe's Ste. Jean River in the midst of the August 1995 heat wave and wore waders every day because the water was so cold.

Still, I really enjoy wet wading and do so often when I fish the Upsalquitch, and even occasionally on the Matapedia. I've found that fleece pants cut off just above the knees work much better than they look. Because they dry so quickly, you don't have to worry about wet car seats, feeling clammy as evening comes on, rashes, or any of the other discomforts associated with wet shorts.

The upper body is more easily taken care of with the usual assortment of shirts, sweaters, and jackets. Because of the protection afforded by chest waders (especially neoprene), I've rarely felt chilly wearing a long-sleeved, zip-neck synthetic undershirt in conjunction with a good wool or chamois shirt. For a rain jacket, I lean toward a light, hooded anorak type. The fewer buttons or zippers a rain jacket has, the better I like it. The most important feature in a rain jacket is the hood, particularly in the area of the chin. Jackets that really keep you dry usually have a drawstring hood and a zippered neck with an inside storm flap. The neck should zip up at least to your chin and preferably well over it.

Salmon fishing icon Lee Wulff is credited with designing the first fishing vest, but I've spent most of my fishing life trying to come up with a better alternative. Like that of many other anglers, my vest tends to become a home for as much stuff as it can hold rather than how much I need. After wearing it for a full day of fishing, I used to get an ache deep in my shoulders. Ultimately I changed to a chest pack—two connected pouches worn like a harness, with one pack in front and one in back.

To me the chest pack is more comfortable than a vest, and it offers almost as much room—more than enough for salmon fishing. The packs sold today are cleverly designed, with plenty of individual pockets in the front pouch and a large, unpartitioned back pouch meant to hold a rain jacket, lunch, and miscellaneous items such as spare spools.

One of the great and lesser-known features of neoprene waders is that their close fit means you can securely tuck fly boxes into their tops, provided you wear a wader belt—which is a good safety idea anyway. And if you replace the wader belt with one of those belt pouches so popular with tourists, you may need nothing else to store your gear. The pouch holds your thermometer, tippet spools, and other things you don't mind getting wet, and your fly boxes stay tucked safely into your waders.

If you do decide on a traditional vest, you'll be much better off with a shorty model that sits up high on your chest than with a conventional-length vest. Salmon flies—particularly expensive traditional salmon flies—are not a pretty sight after they've gotten soaked and subsequently rusted and discolored. Whatever storage and carrying system you choose, try to keep your flies high and dry, wetting them just one at a time. If you do fall in or wade over the pockets of your vest, dry your wet flies under a lightbulb or under your car's heater vent the first chance you get.

ESSENTIALS

Polarized sunglasses are an essential piece of equipment, and the slightly higher price of glass (instead of plastic) lenses is well worth it. I especially like yellow lenses, which make locating fish much easier under overcast skies or low-light conditions. I also like the versatile lightweight plastic glasses that come with interchangeable polarized lenses; these allow you to match ambient light conditions very effectively. Although the optical quality isn't quite comparable to glass, they are modestly priced.

Fishing hats, like most other kinds of hats, have as much to do with the owner's personality as with utility. But whatever style you choose, the underside of the brim should be a nonreflective color (green rather than white, for instance) that's easy on the peripheral vision. If you want to wear a fancy hat with a fleece hatband decorated with all kinds of flies, more power to you. But many of the lowly baseball-style gimme caps have a very useful feature: Their soft foam linings can hold as many flies as a large box. Get those flies wet and you know you've waded where few before you have dared to go!

REELS

In the last chapter I wrote about hooking and losing a large, early-season fish on the Matapedia. Although I'll admit I was unprepared for the strike, the main reason I lost it was equipment related. I hadn't fished my two-handed outfit for some time, and I'd forgotten that that particular reel had such a weak click drag that the spool would overrun with a brisk tug on the line. Okay, I *should* have been aware of that, but I wasn't. I should have palmed the spool gently but I was ham-handed. I may never again make a comparable mistake, but so what? I lost that fish, God bless it.

Right up until the 1980s, many of the popular English single-action reels had that unforgivable flaw, an "adjustable" drag that didn't really adjust, often not even enough to prevent spool overrun. And these were the fancy reels that traditionally dominated the upper end of the market!

Thanks to the explosive growth of American fly fishing and the market-driven changes this wrought in the design of fly reels, even today's lower-end reels have such excellent drag systems that we now face the opposite problem: a drag set too tight at a key moment during hooking and landing. I'll discuss those dangers in chapter 9.

The four things to look for in a salmon reel are *durability, adequate line capacity, a good drag system,* and *an exposed-rim spool* that allows you manually to control the rate at which line is pulled out.

In salmon country, durability counts for a lot because of the usual long trek to the nearest tackle shop. Lightweight reels manufactured from fine metals to exacting tolerances are pretty little instruments, but they don't always take a hit against a rock very well, nor do they always stand up well to the pressure of fighting large salmon in heavy water. Remember, a salmon reel is a tool, not a piece of featherweight jewelry.

At one time salmon anglers had few options between the inexpensive and clunky but extremely durable Pflueger Medalist and the $1,000 handmade Bogdan that you could buy only if you had the right connections. But now excellent fly reels that meet all the criteria of salmon fishing are readily available, thanks in large part to the popularity of saltwater fly fishing.

Line capacity is really a matter of backing capacity. Some reel manufacturers still underestimate the proper amount of backing a spool should carry and advertise reels for 7-weight lines that hold 80 yards of backing. *A suitable spool for salmon fishing should hold no less than 200 yards of backing.* Although 20-pound-test Dacron backing is adequate, its thin diameter can lead to binding and pinching on the spool. If possible, use 30-pound test.

The knot you use to attach the backing to the spool isn't critical, because it should never be tested. If a fish *spools* you (takes all your line and backing), something along the line will usually break before the backing knot. The easiest way to secure the backing to the spool is with a double overhand knot (see fig. 4-1).

The greatest advance in reel engineering over the last decade or so is the availability of quality drag systems on even modestly priced reels. The most popular of these systems, the disc drag, does for the fly reel what its namesake did for automobile brakes. Thanks to this innovation,

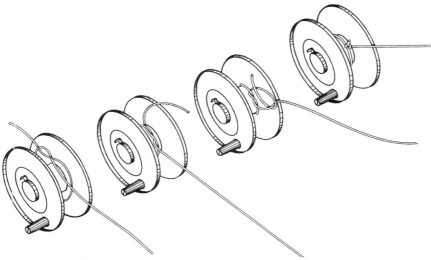

Figure 4-1. Double overhand knot

the basic fly reel has moved one step closer to its cousins, the bait caster and the spinning reel. But instead of eliminating the value of the exposed rim that can be manually controlled, or palmed, the disc system has enhanced it. Trying to futz with a small drag adjustment knob while playing or landing a fish is awkward and risky, and at the very beginning and very end of the process the palming technique is far more reliable and useful than any mechanical drag.

A basic outfit isn't really built around the most prominent components, the rod and reel, but around the line. And while every river and water level will suggest an ideal rod-reel-line combination, the variables dictate that you build your arsenal around a basic outfit.

LINES AND LEADERS

Whether an outfit is light, heavy, or somewhere in between is determined not by the dimensions of the rod but by the weight of line to be cast. Most salmon fishing is done with floating lines of between 7- and 12-weight. I have reservations about using sink-tip lines even where they're allowed or obviously useful (more on this in chapter 11).

The most important feature of a salmon rod is its stiffness, or backbone, and this is directly related to (but not entirely determined by) the

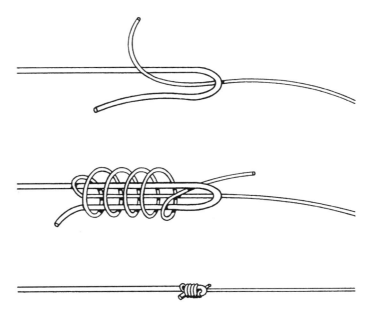

Figure 4-2. Albright knot

line weight the rod is meant to cast. All other things being equal, rods designed for heavier lines must be made stiffer to handle the line's increased casting load. With advances in technology, rod designers have come up with almost infinite variations on this theme, including light-line rods with great backbone. That may seem the best of both worlds; after all, you can land a 25-pound salmon just as easily using a 7-weight line as a 12-weight line.

However, even if a 7-weight has plenty of punch it can be frustrating to fish with it on a windy day on a wide river, even for small grilse, because the line is just too light to cast accurately in a breeze. And remember, you'll often be using large flies. Even during low-water conditions, which often dictate wet flies as small as size 12, you may spend a lot of time fishing with the hardest of all flies to cast—large, wind-resistant dry flies such as the ubiquitous Bomber. Choosing the right line involves more variables than just getting the lightest you can find. Use the Albright knot (see fig. 4-2) to attach your backing to the fly line, and apply a thin coat of flexible cement to the knot to help prevent it from hanging up in your guides when a fish takes you into the backing.

One of the unsung developments of recent years is the fine-tuning of fly-line design. The choice is no longer between double-taper lines, which are easily roll cast and mended during the drift, and weight-forward lines designed to increase casting distance and ease. A variety of underpublicized "long-belly" lines (some specifically designed and labeled for salmon fishing) now feature the casting advantages of a weight-forward line combined with some of the control properties of a double taper. These days, the venerable double-taper line is useful only in conjunction with the increasingly popular two-handed rods, which I'll discuss below.

One thing trout and even steelhead anglers just can't seem to believe about salmon is that the fish aren't at all leader shy, which eliminates an entire area of streamside concern. There may be various reasons why a salmon won't take your fly, but the diameter or visibility of your leader isn't one of them. That's why so many salmon anglers and guides prefer level leaders.

A level length of mono almost entirely eliminates what might be the most devastating of all angling disasters: losing a fish to knot failure. Lose a fish because the fly pulls out, or because you fell in the river and broke your rod following the fish downstream, or because the salmon took you around a sharp rock and severed your leader, and you'll feel keenly disappointed. Lose one because a knot failed and you'll wish you could grind yourself under your own heel. That's because knot failure is the result of laziness or ineptitude on the part of the angler. And some weird natural law dictates that, in retrospect, you always know exactly what happened and why. (Although realistically speaking, you'll often spot a giveaway curlicue, or pig's tail, at the point of your leader, indicating that the leader broke because of a badly tied knot rather than strain.)

While salmon don't seem to give a hoot about your leader, you should—particularly because it can play a subtle part in your success or failure in a variety of ways. These days the newer monofilaments offer almost twice the breaking strength of comparable-diameter mono of just 10 years ago. Anglers conditioned by leader-sensitive fish find this high-strength, thin-diameter combination irresistible. But in salmon fishing its use is limited.

Good casting, in which the leader turns over crisply and the fly lands with no more slack than the angler wishes to produce, maximizes a wet fly's productive "swing" time. Crisp, predictable turnover also allows an angler to fish the dry fly with a specific kind of precision—and confidence—that counts for a lot in salmon fishing. Using the right leader always facilitates good casting, and the right leader for any given situation is determined not by the habits of the salmon but by the size and type of fly being cast, and by the nature of the leader material. A supple, superfine length of 10-pound mono simply won't properly and consistently turn over a size 2 double wet fly or a size 4 Bomber tied on a 4X-long hook.

Salmon may not be leader shy, but they are keenly sensitive to a few other elements of presentation. Delicacy is rarely an issue, because resting salmon seem oblivious to all but the most dramatic and threatening disturbances. But the speed, angle, and consistency at which a wet fly swings or a dry fly drifts are often critical to success. A leader's diameter and relative suppleness play key roles in how readily and quickly a fly achieves the correct swing or drift and in how well it holds that position. A size 8 wet fly tied on a single hook just doesn't "swim" very seductively when tethered to a level piece of stiff 20-pound mono.

For fishing medium to large wet flies (size 8 doubles and larger) and big dry flies, I find that relatively stiff, thick leader material turns over a fly well without interfering with its swing or drift. Maxima, despite its unimpressive diameter-to-strength ratio, is my top choice. Another important but subtle feature of "low-tech" mono is its greater resistance to abrasion compared to the supple new thin-diameter leaders. Because so much of salmon fishing is done on or near the surface, leader abrasion may not seem to be a great factor in salmon fishing, but thorny bushes, rod racks, wooden canoe gunwales, and rocky beaches are all part of salmon fishing, too. Depending on conditions, 9 feet of 12- to 25-pound-test mono will usually do the job.

I prefer to attach a level leader to the fly line with an old-fashioned nail knot (see fig. 4-3) covered with a thin coat of flexible cement. The best tool for making the nail knot is a large sewing needle. As you tighten the knot, make sure the parallel turns of nylon are snug against each other but not overlapping.

The closer you get to the fly end of your line and leader, the more important it is to tie your knots correctly. Two things are important to

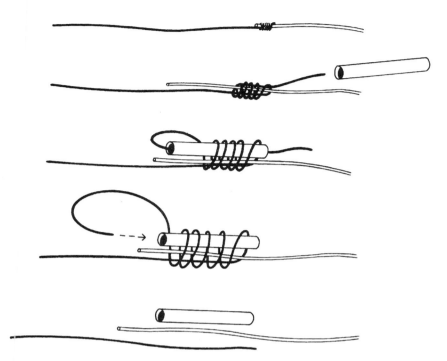

Figure 4-3. Nail knot

remember when tying critical knots: Always wet the knot with saliva before drawing it tight, to eliminate friction that can weaken monofilament; and always leave a short, visible tag end when you trim off excess line. If you don't leave a stub, the tag may pull through and cause the knot to unravel.

The factory-made loop-to-loop connectors built into the tips of some lines are convenient, but they don't always provide the smoothest connection to a leader and can hinge when casting. The best way to check a connection is to grasp the line in one hand and the leader in the other, with the line-leader connection about 8 inches from either hand. Bring your hands together, forcing the line into a standing loop. If the loop forms a smooth arc, there's a good transition from line to leader and your cast should turn over properly.

When I'm using small flies and even a 12-pound-test leader is too heavy, I usually go with a knotless, tapered leader with a single tippet section attached with a surgeon's loop or a blood knot (see figs. 4-4 and 4-5). The surgeon's knot isn't as trim and pretty as a blood knot, but it's much

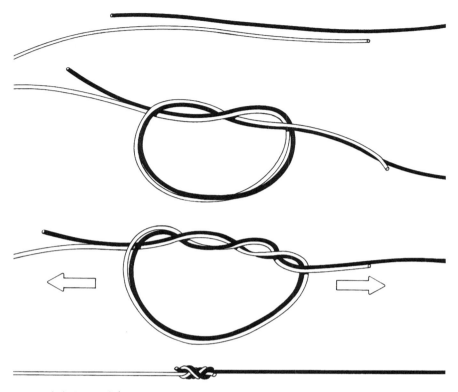

Figure 4-4. Surgeon's knot

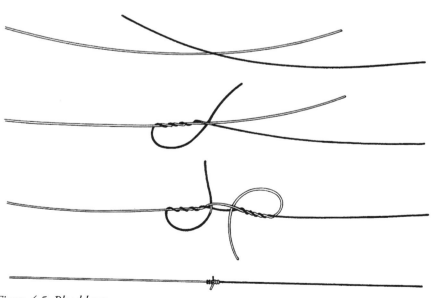

Figure 4-5. Blood knot

easier to tie, it's stronger, and it can successfully connect lines of significantly different diameters. I use the surgeon's loop exclusively, but if you insist on using a blood knot be sure that you make your turns at each end of the knot in opposite directions, so that the tag ends form a tiny cross at right angles to the leader opposite (rather than alongside) each other.

I use a tapered leader when fishing small flies, for a number of reasons. Although delicacy of presentation isn't a critical issue most of the time, it becomes more important when fishing fine—and it certainly doesn't hurt to cast and fish as smoothly and gently as possible. Also, there comes a point when the drastic difference in diameter between the fly line and a level leader creates an impediment to casting and presentation.

Ultrathin mono does excel when used with small wet flies (size 8 and smaller) and dry flies in low water. If it's part of a tapered leader, you get the best of both worlds: enough butt to turn over an air-resistant fly, and a thin, limp tippet that allows a fly to swim or float unimpeded.

One last important thing to remember about leaders: Inspect them for wind knots, nicks, or kinks each morning before you fish. Monofilament is cheap. Tie on a fresh leader or a new tippet after every fish caught, or every other day.

RODS

When it comes to rods I'm a big fan of balance and of using the appropriate gear instead of trying to perform impressive stunts or worming my way into the light-tackle column of the record books. This is partly an ethical decision, because landing a salmon quickly without horsing it puts less stress on the fish. But I also learned the value of fishing with the proper gear on a wild night on the Upsalquitch many years ago.

At the time I was the proverbial novice for whom a little knowledge was a dangerous thing. And I was a member of a generation that took its cues from Lee Wulff, then an ardent advocate of light-tackle fishing. Lee was also an adventurous soul who delighted in accomplishing feats of angler derring-do that others thought impossible—and for most people they *were* impossible. Among other things, Lee caught salmon using just the tip section of a light bamboo trout rod, and he also caught salmon on size 20 dry flies.

I knew the Upsalquitch had a strong grilse run, so I decided one July that it would be great fun to catch a grilse with a 9-foot, 6-weight trout rod. When Paul Nevin and I arrived at Tucker's camp in time for the evening fishing, it had been raining most of the day. The river was rising steadily, but it was still clear. Paul and I were assigned to fish that evening with Ollie Marshall in Mouth Pool, just above the confluence of the Restigouche and Upsalquitch, at the upstream end of a 100-yard stretch of swift whitewater.

Mouth Pool is a good transitional resting area above this heavy water—the first possible stop for salmon ascending the Upsalquitch. It's also thought that the occasional brutish Restigouche fish takes a wrong turn and briefly holds in Mouth Pool before dropping back down and continuing up the Restigouche.

It was a mysterious, spectacular evening for fishing. Dark thunderheads rolled by overhead, producing intermittent rain. Between showers, banks of fog drifted like torn white cloth across the hillsides, and the sharp smell of wet pine irradiated the air. At medium water level in those days, Mouth Pool consisted of only about 30 yards of fishable water, all along the west bank; that day, however, the high water gave us twice as much to fish. The flow was so strong that the anchor barely held the canoe even at the very top of the pool, and the craft rocked threateningly in the swift, rolling water as we began to fish.

I was using a Banker, a fly I had made up and named for my buddy Chris von Strasser. I was casting only about 10 feet of line on the very first drop (by boat, a pool is always fished from a succession of anchored positions called *drops*) when a big fish took with a great splash that caught us by surprise. The little rod bent sharply, and I could feel the full weight of the fish in my forearm. A moment later, however, the fly pulled out. Shaken, I fished out the drop with no further action, and Paul fished the next drop without moving a salmon.

On my second drop, I had about 25 feet of line out when a salmon took with a solid, slow pull at the end of the swing. This fish was solidly hooked, and Ollie scrambled to fire up the outboard and head for shore. The fish turned and headed downstream toward the standing waves leading into the Restigouche. I felt utterly helpless as Ollie motored in, the 6-weight bent practically into a closed loop in my hand. As we reached shore, I began to pump the little rod and gain line. Something didn't seem quite right, although with a full fly line and 100 yards of backing out in the river I didn't know what it was. But with each turn of the reel it became more obvious: I had lost the fish long before; the weight I felt was merely that of the river tugging at all that slack line, putting a deep bend in my light stick.

Granted, I might have lost those two fish on *any* kind of tackle. But that rod simply didn't have enough backbone either to sink the hook solidly into the jaw of a big fish in heavy water or to apply sufficient pressure to one that was decently hooked. Since then I've caught both MSW salmon and grilse on a 6-weight outfit, but under those conditions it was stupid to fish with very light tackle. I remember the events of that evening as if they occurred just yesterday, and they taught me early on that underestimating a river is just as foolish as underestimating a salmon.

For years the basic salmon fishing rod was the *9-by-9*—a 9-foot, single-handed rod designed to cast a 9-weight line. This is still the best all-purpose rig, even though engineers have since designed light 10-foot rods for 8- and even 7-weight lines that offer plenty of backbone along with superior potential for finesse. But a 9-by-9 still turns over a large or air-resistant fly better, especially in a breeze. It's a rough-and-ready, versatile tool.

While the extra foot of length offered by a 10-foot rod can come in very handy, especially for the wading angler, using such a rod all day while wading a big river such as the Miramichi or Matapedia can be tiring.

One of the most significant developments of the past few years has been the rediscovery of the two-handed rod, which has always been the norm for salmon fishing in the British Isles. Although the ponderous split-cane two-handers shed a lot of weight in the change to graphite, most of them were still designed to cast 11- and 12-weight lines. Under low-water conditions, such lines land on the surface like a hawser, so the two-hander was strictly a rod for big water and big wet flies. But recently a handful of manufacturers have started to produce light two-handers designed to cast lines as fine as 8-weight. These rods, which range from 11 to 16 feet in length, are undoubtedly the best tools for wet-fly fishing of any kind on big rivers, no matter what the water level.

Two-handers enable an angler to cast great distances with surprisingly little effort. This has less to do with the length of the rod than with the power and authority lent to it by the use of two hands. Even an experienced American salmon angler who has never tried a two-hander may be astonished by some of the advantages of using both arms.

Traditionally two-handers were always used with double-taper lines, which roll cast a country mile and allow the angler to use a double roll cast, known as the *spey cast,* when a backcast was impossible because of riparian topography. In fact, most British experts with the two-hander rarely backcast, even when the terrain allows them to do so.

But innovative Yanks, with their mania for light tackle—and false casting—put the two-hander to use in a different way, concentrating on the long rod's pure power as a casting tool. Loading their reels with weight-forward lines, they discovered that with just one backcast they could shoot line great distances, enabling them to cover a lot more water, a lot more quickly, than they ever could with a one-handed rod.

Although weight-forward lines shoot better and farther, at times the roll cast or even the spey cast comes in handy. Both are relatively easy to learn (in fact the rank novice will learn even the simple two-step overhead cast much more easily with a two-hander). So if you have only one spool for your reel, load it with a double-taper line.

Because of its superior casting reach, the two-hander allows you to fish from a much more comfortable wading depth. In fact it's awkward to use a two-hander if you wade deeper than waist level. The typical two-hander's long handle is also convenient. You can just jam the butt into your midsection as you fish out the cast, time and again. All this adds up to one very important practical advantage: A two-hander *greatly* reduces angler fatigue.

While two-handers have some formidable advantages, they also have some drawbacks. They aren't great tools for dry-fly fishing, particularly for less experienced anglers. Because of their length, two-handers aren't well suited to fishing a short line or working on fish from a close position. And when fishing from a boat on all but the biggest rivers, or while wading in medium to small rivers under low-water conditions, using even the lightest of two-handers can amount to overkill.

Because most dry-fly fishing is done well into the season in medium to low water, 7- and 8-weight lines matched with stiff rods (backbone becomes increasingly important as you go down in line weight) are usually the best choices. Ideally, smaller, lighter flies fished in low water ought to be presented with lighter lines, which contribute to casting accuracy and enhance fly movement. But a rod that offers good control of the cast under *most* conditions is preferable to one that will lay down a light line and a small fly with minimal disturbance under *ideal* conditions. For that reason I like a 10-foot rod for an 8-weight line best of all, even though it can be more awkward than a shorter rod when casting a short line or when fishing a dry fly from a boat to fish just 15 or 20 feet away.

If could have only one outfit, it would be the reliable 9-by-9. But if I could—or had to—keep two rigs, I would have a 14-foot two-hander for an 11-weight line and a 10-foot one-hander for an 8-weight.

CHAPTER 5

The Flies

Classic featherwing wet flies, developed and refined on the salmon rivers of the British Isles, are the crown jewels of the sport—powerful symbols of all that is refined, elegant, and intriguingly arcane about fly fishing. A properly tied featherwing salmon fly is such a pretty and complicated thing that many people who never even go salmon fishing tie them. It doesn't hurt that salmon flies have evocative and colorful names such as the Jock Scott, Mar Lodge, Lady Amherst, Nighthawk, Hairy Mary, and Durham Ranger.

The first thing a prospective salmon fisher should do is buy a dozen of these gorgeous, traditional flies from an accomplished fly tyer. Mount them on tan felt in a gilt-framed shadowbox, hang it in a prominent place, then order a bunch of hairwing flies with names like the Rusty Rat. These are what you'll actually use fishing.

Okay, I'm exaggerating. But not by much. Even the borderline aesthetes among my salmon fishing buddies rarely use featherwing flies, and they almost never use those fully dressed patterns that have been such an effective public relations tool for fly fishing. This is not because featherwing flies are in any way inferior. On the contrary, most of the common hairwing flies either imitate or resemble traditional featherwing patterns. And many of those complex, fully dressed featherwings seem to swim with an extra dose of that elusive, highly coveted quality we loosely call life. It wasn't just for purely aesthetic reasons that their creators used so many layers of colorful and patterned feathers.

But salmon fishing on both sides of the Atlantic is tradition driven, and the salmon anglers of the New World were bound to develop their own. Many traditional British featherwings include 15 or more components, often rare or difficult to acquire. It wasn't easy keeping a full kit of such materials on hand in the colonies. Besides, who needed feathers from the rare South American blue chatterer when fox and bear fur provided good and readily available winging materials?

Ultimately hairwing flies—using fewer and more common materials and fabricated in half as many steps as most featherwings—came to define the Canadian tradition. But the populist explosion of fly fishing has brought another trend: Anglers are flying by the seats of their pants, incorporating various synthetic materials, reducing classic hairwings even further than the hairwings reduced the featherwings, and making up new patterns. When you're making flies for yourself, instead of the Lord of the Manor with his grand taste and nitpicky demands, it's an entirely different ball game.

One thing's for sure: Salmon don't care one way or the other. Fly selection is the most mystifying facet of salmon fishing, but what do you expect when the goal is to tempt a fasting fish to eat? Ultimately much of fly selection is pure habit, some is whimsy, and the part that is rational isn't exactly rocket science.

Featherwing flies work very nicely on this side of the Atlantic, and hairwings and dry flies work fine in the British Isles—or they would, if only those folks would deign to use them. Generally they won't, in part because of all the tradition-bound mumbo-jumbo that surrounds fly selection. Fished day in, day out, the British Stoat's Tail and the Canadian Black Bear, Green Butt, would probably outproduce any other salmon flies. But what fun would that be? And what would you talk about over cocktails at the lodge?

For a number of years Chris von Strasser leased a prime beat on the Naver, a first-class river in Scotland. The other anglers and *gillies* (guides) insisted that Scottish salmon won't take dry flies, or even most of those gauche Canadian flies. One year during Chris's week the water was so low and warm that it was almost impossible to get a good swing from a wet fly in most pools. The salmon were holed up and stale, disinclined to take anything as they awaited a rise of water.

Unwilling to absorb a skunking like all the other rods, Chris began fishing with outlandish Canadian dry flies and wet flies such as the Green Machine, a small, buoyant fly resembling a tapered green cork. These were so effective that by the end of the week, a small entourage of sports and gillies was trailing Chris around, convinced he was taking his fish by some illegal means.

Even in Canada, where anglers are more freewheeling and experimental, many will tell you that certain types or patterns of flies don't produce on their rivers. Guides in particular can be hidebound this way, and their conservatism pitted against a sport's desire to experiment can present formidable diplomatic problems. But in my experience the main component in fly productivity is most often the frequency which with it's used.

At the same time it would be silly to ignore recorded evidence proving the efficiency of one fly or another, or the general agreement that certain colors work better on certain rivers than on others. Undeniably, productivity is one of the few quantifiable factors in the arena of fly selection. For example, the Miramichi is undoubtedly a green river, the Restigouche is a gold and silver one, and Penobscot anglers fare well on the Halloween combination of black and orange.

SALMON FLY CRITERIA

Flies are usually discussed as individual patterns, but I wouldn't overemphasize specific identity when building a good, basic fly collection that will fit into one box. There are four different factors (listed below in descending order of importance) to consider about a salmon fly before you even think about what specific patterns to carry and use.

The first factor is *hook size,* which is usually determined by water clarity and level. The next is *hook style*—double, single, or something

Fly tying during the midday break is commonplace at most salmon camps (Photo: Val Atkinson)

unusual, such as a tube fly. The third is *density*—the amount of material used in dressing the fly. The final issue is general *tint*—dark, bright, or colorful.

Some experts will consider it heretical to place tint last on this list, but there's a reason for that beyond a paucity of hard evidence suggesting it should be placed higher. The other factors combine to determine what the salmon see and how they see it. Optimizing your chances in those areas makes it more likely that *any* pattern will be successful. Then it's simply a matter of substitution until you hit on the "right" pattern, or some other factor forces you to reconsider the whole situation.

Granted, you don't go through this process like an automaton ticking out calculations, and even if you do, you rarely pick a fly and—bang!—catch a salmon. But thinking first about these four issues, instead of about Green Highlanders or Conrads or Silver Rats, brings salmon fishing a little closer to roulette than to Russian roulette, which is about as certain as it gets. Let's take a closer look at each of these four criteria, in the order in which you should consider them.

HOOK SIZE

A wet fly's size should be dictated by water level, water clarity, and the nature of the river. In the early season you often fish with flies as large as size 2 doubles (or 1/0 or 2/0 singles); as the water drops you may go down as low as size 10 or even 12 singles. Never assume that a fly is too small. One of the rare reliable truths of salmon fishing is that far more big salmon are caught by going to smaller flies than to bigger ones; even size 12 and 14 specialized salmon hooks are strong enough to hold large fish. Generally, you'll do most of your fishing with hooks ranging from size 2 to size 8.

HOOK STYLE

Doubles versus singles has always been one of salmon fishing's livelier debates, encompassing such issues as whether two hooks hold a fish better than one. Don't worry about that: A well-hooked fish is just as secure on a single hook as on a double, and a poorly hooked fish can be lost even on a treble. A number of factors are far more important in determining how well a fish is hooked, including angler competence and simple luck.

Generally, double hooks seem to balance hairwing flies in a way that gives them a pleasing, effective swing. A Rusty Rat is probably most effective when it's chug-chugging doggedly through swift water, stabilized by twin hooks that act as miniature outriggers. Conversely, the ethereal quality of featherwings is enhanced by the use of lighter, finer single hooks. A Jock Scott tied on a single hook sweeping through a glassine run isn't merely classic, it's deadly.

It's critically important to match the type of hook you choose to the water you're fishing. Even during low water, the rolling run at the head of a pool may be swift enough to force a featherwing single to sputter on the surface, or to spin and helicopter as it's swept along. Such runs are always fished more effectively with doubles, even tiny ones. Conversely, a double may be too hook-heavy to swing nicely through the flat, slower water at the tail of the same pool. Generally, rough or very swift water calls for doubles, while flatter or slower water is suited to light, high-riding flies tied on single hooks.

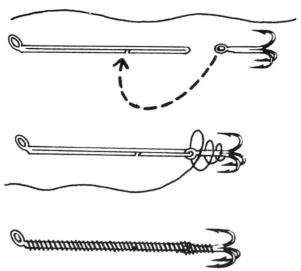

Figure 5-1. Waddington shank with treble

A number of specialized hook configurations are used in salmon fishing, such as the Esmond Drury treble, which is used in making tiny flies, or the Waddington shank, which features a treble attached via a piece of stiff monofilament to a straight shank on which the body of the fly is tied (see fig. 5-1). If you do end up using specialized hooks, check local regulations to make sure they're legal.

The last significant hook variation is the longer, lighter hook used in tying *low-water patterns,* which usually are tied on only the front half of the hook shank—in other words, a size 12 fly tied on a size 6 hook. Low-water patterns have always been popular in Britain, but less so here, partly because North American anglers are perfectly willing to fish with wet flies tied on tiny hooks.

On this side of the Atlantic, low-water double hooks are often used instead of traditional doubles in tying full-bodied flies. Many experienced anglers feel that the slim, low-water doubles create more natural-looking flies. The drawback is that the lighter-weight hooks make it harder to keep the fly riding under the surface in swift, high water.

It's too bad that the classic low-water single is relatively unpopular here, because the salmon don't seem to mind all that naked metal. With low-water hooks you can use heavier leaders, and the dressing-to-metal ratio gives low-water flies a pleasing weight that helps them swim with more authority in swift water than standard small flies. Low-water flies can also achieve more of a bewitchingly sparse effect than flies tied on short, stubby hooks.

DENSITY

As a rule—one that novice fly tyers and fly buyers almost never understand—sparse dressings are the most effective. Heavily dressed flies may look more impressive or appear to offer more bang for the buck, but they rarely work as well. The only advantage heavily dressed flies have is weight. They sink faster and ride lower, which may come in handy under high-water conditions.

TINT

One of the grand old saws of salmon fishing is: "Bright day, bright fly; dark day, dark fly." This maxim works about half the time, and you needn't know much about odds to understand what that means. But it contains a great hidden rule: It's always better to begin fishing with a theory and then spend your time systematically confirming or disproving it. Any game plan is better than no game plan; even the silliest brings structure and focus to your fishing. Although salmon fishing is not an empirical pursuit, it is kindest to those who go about it somewhat empirically. Some anglers always catch more fish, and it isn't just because they're lucky.

I mentioned earlier that, in a long-term contest, a mostly black fly would probably outfish any other pattern or color. This may be because black changes less in appearance over a wide range of ambient conditions. It's even possible that, under some circumstances, such as when the sun is bright and directly overhead, a salmon sees *all* flies as more or less black.

So don't be so eager to declare yourself the new Lee Wulff after you catch a big salmon on a Silver Rat when nobody else in camp did anything that day using the recommended black flies. Your salmon may have seen something that looked to it a lot more like a Black Rat than a silver one.

Just a little something to think about.

While mostly black flies seem to be the most effective most of the time and often draw strikes from apparently disinterested fish, bright flies seem slightly more effective at convincing interested but reluctant fish to take the fly. I've often had this theory validated on hot, bright days with low water, one of the most difficult times for salmon fishing.

Distinguishing between bright and colorful flies may seem confusing, but there is a significant, defining difference between them: Bright flies have predominantly tinsel bodies, which gives them loads more flash. They're often used on bright days because the sunlight brings out the tinsel's deadly twinkle. Colorful flies, including such standbys as the green and yellow Cosseboom, the Rusty Rat, and the Miramichi Butterfly, are versatile, all-day flies. Each river boasts a favorite, the one almost everyone uses. Keep it at the top of your list, even if a real or imagined inside source (such as the recent entries in the camp log book, or the opinion of some guy you met in a tackle shop) suggests otherwise.

Just why an angler would spend the morning prospecting with a colorful Green Highlander rather than a Black Bear, Green Butt is something I'm hard put to answer, but that's what most people do. Perhaps a black fly's somberness makes it less appealing to the angler, if not to the salmon. The colorful fly looks more cheery, more optimistic. Human reasoning also suggests that the colorful fly is more eye-catching and thus more likely to trigger a strike from curious, playful, or aggressive fish.

But let's say that you're not prospecting—you're fishing a run that holds salmon and can be fished through with a wet fly in 15 or 20 minutes. Circumstances permitting, I would fish through the run with at least three different wet flies, then with one large and one small dry fly.

For my first fly I'd choose the one in which I have the most confidence under the conditions. Early in the morning, before the light hits the water, I'd fish a predominantly black fly. Later in the day, if the sun wasn't too bright, I'd fish a colorful fly first. Under a bright sun I'd use a bright fly. I'd then fish through with the second most likely fly suggested by the conditions, and so on.

ESSENTIAL WET FLIES

With all these things in mind let's put together a collection, starting with wet flies. We're aiming for variety in pattern, size, and style, and you can achieve this with as few as six wet-fly patterns. If you carry these flies, and add examples of the most productive fly on the given river you'll be fishing, you should be in good shape.

A word about alternate dressings: Fly-tying anglers often "customize" classic dressings, changing almost any component, and reducing or adding to the classic ingredients. Even traditional sources often give conflicting recipes for fly tyers. My own sourcebooks include the indispensable, acknowledged classic, Colonel Joseph D. Bates Jr.'s *Atlantic Salmon Flies and Fishing* (Stackpole, Mechanicsburg, Pennsylvania, 1970 and 1996), and Poul Jorgenson's *Salmon Flies* (Stackpole, 1978).

Substitute materials can be used (up to a point) with no real loss of efficiency. If you don't have black bear hair, calf tail or squirrel tail dyed black works fine. Sometimes you may have to substitute because of restrictions on materials from threatened or endangered species. Reductions make the most sense in a fly's tail area, where there may be as many as four or five components, some or all of which can be eliminated without altering the basic nature of the fly.

Personalizing classic dressings is one of those whatever-turns-you-on things. It's pretty harmless, unless you alter one or more of a fly's key components. There are countless variations on the Black Bear, Green Butt, and the fact that they all work proves that it's pretty hard to screw up something so good.

BLACK BEAR, GREEN BUTT

Thread	Black
Tag	Oval silver tinsel
Butt	Fluorescent green floss
Tail	Golden pheasant crest
Body	Black floss
Rib	Oval silver tinsel
Wing	Black bear hair
Hackle	Black hen, tied collar-style
Head	Black thread

This fly is the salmon angler's equivalent of the trendy woman's little black cocktail dress. It's just as simple, versatile, and effective.

Carry the Black Bear, Green Butt, in a variety of sizes; the low-water dressings are particularly deadly. In small sizes, the tail is often eliminated. Some people prefer a red butt to a green one and swear that it makes a difference. If you want to use a black fly with a little more pizzazz in its original form, consider the Black Dose, the Nighthawk, and the Undertaker, all-star variations on the black-fly theme.

SILVER RAT

Thread	Red
Tag	Fine oval gold tinsel
Body	Flat silver tinsel
Ribbing	Oval silver tinsel
Wing	Mixed black and white bucktail
Sides	Jungle cock
Hackle	Grizzly, tied collar-style
Head	Red tying thread

The various rats—Rusty, Black, Gold, Gray, Copper, and Blue— constitute the first family of North American salmon flies. The colorful Rusty Rat may have caught more salmon than any other hairwing fly. But I think the family's real superstar is the one that so many Canadian guides pick when they want to fish a "bright" fly: the Silver Rat.

I've never done well with the Silver Rat in large sizes, although I don't doubt that others have. After all, shiny spinners and spoons have accounted for scads of salmon in the British Isles. But in size 2 and larger, dark or colorful flies seem plenty visible to me. When the water is dirty as well as high, flies made with copper instead of silver tinsel are often effective. In low water the Silver Rat is outstanding in medium to small doubles and singles, when its twinkle is eye-catching but not overpowering.

The classic Silver Rat is a wonderful example of how creatively fly tyers can complicate a relatively simple concept. This is a fly whose lowly bucktail wing evolved into one of gray fox—with guard hairs mixed in. The "official" substitute for the fox hair wing is hair from the tail of a monga ringtail monkey!

But I've fished Silver Rats tied using only three ingredients—black thread, a body of silver tinsel, and a wing of natural gray squirrel tail—and they work. In fact, Shane Mann ties this reduced version and hooks many salmon each season on the Upsalquitch, particularly when using small sizes (8 and 10).

Other excellent bright flies include the recently neglected but amply proven Silver Gray, and the reduced hairwing versions of two feather-wing classics, the Dusty Miller and the Silver Doctor. An excellent bright fly with absolutely no snob appeal is that old trout angler's standby, the Mickey Finn streamer (the wing is tied short in the salmon version).

GREEN HIGHLANDER

Thread	Black
Tag	Fine oval tinsel and yellow floss
Tail	Golden pheasant crest
Butt	Black ostrich herl
Body	Rear quarter, yellow floss; remainder, bright green seal fur or Seal-Ex dubbing
Ribbing	Oval silver tinsel
Wing	Small bunch of yellow, orange, and green polar bear hair, covered with natural brown bucktail as a main wing
Hackle	Grass green, over seal fur portion of body
Throat	Bright yellow hackle, tied collar-style
Sides	Jungle cock
Head	Black thread

Here in the most crowded and spectacular category, colored flies, the best fly is a toss-up between the Cosseboom, the Rusty Rat, and the Green Highlander. But consider this: The green and yellow color combination may be the most popular and deadly of them all. In fact, the Rusty Rat, with its gold and coppery green body, and the Cosseboom, whose body is a combination of yellow floss and green African goat, both echo the original theme boldly stated by the mother of all colored flies, the Green Highlander.

This is an excellent fly in all sizes, and there are endless variations on the complicated and elegant original featherwing dressing. In low water, a simple version with a body of translucent green dubbing picked out to look shaggy, a very sparse brown wing, and a single turn of yellow hackle has been productive for me.

The traditional featherwings include some of the most dazzling of all the colored flies.

BUTTERFLY

Thread	Black
Tail	Red hackle fibers
Body	Bronze peacock herl
Wing	White calf tail, divided in equal bunches and secured at about a 25-degree angle to the body
Hackle	Brown, collar-style

This sui generis wet fly could easily be a top choice as a colored fly, but it has earned a place of its own because of its unique wing. If you pump the rod as the fly swings through a drift, the Butterfly's wing configuration makes the fly pulse, and at times salmon find this action irresistible. The fly has a lot of life, which is the highest of endorsements. In a dead drift through fairly slow water, the Butterfly hangs in an apparent state of suspension better than most traditionally winged wet flies. And it's the *only* popular wet fly with a white wing. The Butterfly's quite a package.

It works best in medium to small sizes. The planing effect of the wing demands the use of double hooks to keep the fly submerged in swift water. In low or smooth water, a light-wire single hook allows for the maximum pulsing effect, with the fly swimming close to the surface. Sometimes I dress the wing with flotant so that when the fly speeds up at the end of its swing, it actually breaks the surface and makes an enticing wake; sometimes this goads fish into striking. The wing and the properties it gives the fly make low-water dressings unimportant.

Oddly enough, there are no popular variations on the Butterfly. Maybe this is the first time salmon anglers have obeyed the rule, "If it ain't broke, don't fix it." But I've got to confess that we had good success on the

Upsalquitch for a few years with a Butterfly variation we dubbed the Buttercup, which lacked the red tail and had a green body with a yellow split wing. Naturally, the guides soon shortened its name to the B-Cup.

GREEN MACHINE

Thread	Black
Butt	Red wool
Body	Clipped green deer hair
Hackle	Brown, palmered through the body

This relatively recent creation is appropriately if not romantically named. It's a fish-catching machine, plain and simple, with a distinguished albeit obscure lineage that contains obvious blood ties to the venerable Bomber dry fly. The properly tied Green Machine has a graceful reverse taper on a double hook, with the body narrowing slightly toward the hook eye.

Although the Green Machine is seldom fished in large sizes (the buoyancy of the deer hair makes it difficult to keep the fly below the surface in high, fast water), it excels in all other sizes and hook configurations, particularly size 8 and 10 doubles. Because of the clipped deer hair body's inherent bulk, low-water dressings aren't especially useful. There are many variations on the Green Machine (including the blue-bodied Smurf), but the original is still tops.

WILD CARDS

This isn't a category of flies but a catchall heading designed to make things a little bit more fun for you, and to allow me to mention a few flies that aren't easily classified as dark, bright, or colorful.

BLACK AND BLUE

Thread	Black
Tag	Gold wire
Tail	Three peacock sword fibers

Body	Flat silver tinsel
Wing	Black calf tail
Hackle	Kingfisher blue, tied collar-style
Head	Black thread

Okay, it's vain of me to include a fly that I designed in this august company, but the Black and Blue has really worked for me. It has also worked for Jim Emery, who—with his usual attention to detail—has incorporated changes that I'm sure represent improvements over the original. These include a pheasant crest tail, an underwing of blue hackle, and a body of jazzy "holographic spectra tinsel." As long as you're working with the black wing–blue hackle foundation, you can't go far wrong.

Number this fly among some other fine patterns, including the Sweep and the legendary Blue Charm, based on the very effective but (at least in North America) not very popular combination of black and blue.

The Black and Blue itself may be effective because it not only uses this proven color combination but also comes closer than any other pattern I know to touching all three types of tint (black, bright, colorful) without looking—or fishing—like a forced hybrid. It fishes well under a variety of light conditions and in all sizes and styles. It lacks only the ringing endorsement of the multitudes.

THE TUBE FLY

You won't find many women wearing brooches made of tube flies, and you won't find the flies emblazoned on coasters or china platters. The tube fly looks like a small hank of dog hair tied together at one end. Even the most astute angler is hard put to explain how a fly so simple can be so devastating.

The tube fly is tied by covering a length of hollow plastic tubing with some body material (such as floss ribbed with tinsel), then tying in a sparse overlayer of hair at the front of the tube and all around it. The angler threads his leader through the tube and ties on his hook (usually a double), the eye of which he then pushes gently into the back end of the tube. Because it weighs far less than a conventional fly of comparable length, even a large tube fly can be cast easily. More important, these big flies are so light and slender that they swim and skate and make wakes through the water in a way that salmon often love. But small tubes also work well.

Most people agree that the tube fly's long, slender shape is a fair imitation of a tiny eel or any number of slim baitfish that are part of the adult salmon's diet. Thus a salmon in fresh water may strike at a tube fly because of its familiar shape, even though the salmon isn't really interested in eating.

Almost any conventional pattern can be tied on a tube in a reduced form. You can't go far wrong with a Black Bear, Green Butt, tube, but to add variety try the Hairy Mary Tube. It's made with a body of black floss ribbed with silver tinsel and a wing of mixed fox squirrel tail and blue-dyed gray squirrel tail.

I've experimented a lot with flies that I loosely call "eel" flies; these are attempts to duplicate the tube fly on conventional, long-shank, light-wire hooks. One has produced well enough to become a favorite. It's a simple tie using black thread, a red tag, and a body of Krystal Chenille. The key is an extra-long wing of brown bear hair fixed near the eye, but with one clump of fibers above the shank and one below. This style of wing is less likely to foul around the bend than an extra-long wing tied in the traditional way. An alternative is to tie the wing in at the head, as a tail, and to make a short, stubby body.

MUDDLER MINNOW

Thread	Black
Tail	Mottled turkey quill segments
Body	Flat gold tinsel
Wing	Gray squirrel tail, with mottled turkey atop
Head	Spun and clipped natural deer hair
Overwing	A few strands of hair from the head, left long

Like the Mickey Finn, this trout fly has found a niche in salmon fishing. The Muddler is a plug-ugly fly, which is probably why some anglers don't use it. Others swear by it.

The Muddler works well on double hooks in large to medium sizes (2 through 8) in spite—or because—of its distinctive clipped deer hair head. That head allows you to fish the Muddler as a dry fly on the appropriate hook. I especially like the Muddler as a waking fly used in conjunction with a technique called the riffling hitch, which I'll cover in chapter 10.

DRY FLIES

Dry flies, and the basic strategy for their selection, are less complicated than wet flies. This is not only because there are far fewer dry-fly patterns but also because most effective dry-fly fishing is done to visible fish, and presentation is far more important than pattern.

Consider this: A dry-fly angler can properly work a visible salmon with five or six different flies and know where he stands with that fish in about 20 minutes. The wet-fly angler, combing an 80-yard-long pool that contains one invisible salmon, may take about two hours to fish through with just three flies. Furthermore, almost every cast the dry-fly angler makes will more or less cover the fish, while in two hours of wet-fly fishing the angler may make only three casts that swim closely enough to the salmon with each of his flies. This reduces his effective fishing time to only a few precious minutes.

Of course that's one of the reasons the minutiae of wet-fly selection can be so important.

In fact the four factors you should consider for choosing a wet fly are either irrelevant or only marginally important for dry-fly fishing. There is no effective rule of thumb concerning dry-fly size. Dry flies are rarely productive during high water (partly because the fish lie deep, and cold temperatures make them reluctant to rise), while in low water even small grilse will often respond enthusiastically to the largest of dry flies.

There is only one kind of dry-fly hook, a light single, although shank length can vary by pattern, especially with long-bodied flies such as the Bomber. The "classic" recipe calls for a hook of size 2 or 4, with a 4X-long shank. Many veteran anglers now like all their dry flies tied in extra-wide-gap hooks. Fly density varies much less in dry flies, because all of them must have enough hackle to float. Tint or color *is* a definite factor, but in an arbitrary way rather than in relation to ambient conditions.

This doesn't mean that you can't get into a rip-snorting, two-hour debate over the split wing versus the clump wing on the Bomber, if that suits your temperament. It just suggests that dry-fly fishing gives you the opportunity to decide the issue in a much more satisfying and reliable way—by showing both versions to a salmon, and letting the fish have the last word. And *his* last word may vary from day to day.

Three patterns will give you enough range to effectively fish dry flies.

BOMBER

Thread	Black
Tail	Clump of white calf tail
Body	Spun and clipped natural deer hair, tapered at both ends
Wing	Clump of white calf tail, extending forward of the eye at about a 45-degree upward angle
Hackle	Brown, palmered through the body

Count the remarkable effectiveness of the Bomber as just another one of those mysteries of salmon fishing. Go fishing without a black wet fly in your box and you're making a mistake. Go dry-fly fishing without a Bomber and you're crazy.

The Bomber's alleged inspiration was a salmon that swirled angrily on a discarded cigar butt—probably the only wet cigar that was ever of inestimable value. The more conventional story of the Bomber's origin is that one Father Elmer Smith, fishing for seatrout on the Royal River in Yarmouth, Maine, saw a kid hammering salmon when the local hotshots were getting skunked. The boy was using a huge, ratty deer hair mouse. Smith began to toy with the concept, eventually slimming down the body to make it easier to cast and adding hackle to bulk it back up (a grizzly hackle dyed red). He first fished it as a wet fly in the 1960s on the Miramichi at Russell Rapids near Doaktown. Since he noticed that fish often struck when it was in the film, he added two stiff saddle hackles, greased the body, and began fishing it as a dry fly.

In any event, I'd rather have the Bomber in various sizes and colors than an assortment of other dry flies. Different color combinations have become very popular, including orange body–white wing–brown hackle (a personal favorite); green body–yellow wing–yellow hackle; and white body–red hackle–white wing. Some anglers also like the wing upright and divided. Get the natural and at least two other color combinations, in medium to large sizes. There is no wet fly too small for a salmon to take and no Bomber too large.

THE BUCK BUG

Thread	Black
Tail	Fox squirrel tail
Body	Spun and clipped natural deer hair
Rib	Brown saddle hackle, palmered through body
Hackle	Brown, tied full

The Buck Bug is an excellent small dry fly (sizes 6 to 10). It can be very effective on fish that have already seen one or more large dries. I prefer some of the variations on the classic Buck Bug, particularly when I've already shown the fish similar—albeit larger—Bombers. I especially like the green Buck Bug, which is essentially a dry Green Machine with a short tuft of red wool for a tail (instead of a tag) and a single hackle palmered through the body.

ROYAL WULFF

Thread	Black
Tail	Brown bucktail
Body	Peacock herl with a red floss center band
Wing	White calf tail, upright and divided
Hackle	Brown, tied full

Standard trout dry flies often work on salmon, and it's surprising how small a fly a large salmon will take. I like the Royal Wulff because of its colors, which are similar to those of that effective wet fly, the Butterfly.

The White and Gray Wulffs, members of the same family, are also good. Other trout flies that salmon will take include large stonefly imitations such as the Golden Stonefly.

The Humpy, a popular trout fly in the Rockies, is also said to be an excellent salmon fly. It has a yellow body and a brown and grizzly hackle, with a tail, back, and upright split wing of deer hair. All that deer hair gives the Humpy excellent flotation, which is a great plus in a game that sometimes involves making 15 or 20 quick presentations without a single false cast. The Humpy can be tied using typical salmon color combinations in body and hackle (green and yellow, orange and white, and so on) without compromising the fly's unique design. It is a popular dry fly on the Miramichi.

KNOTS

Now that you have the flies, you need only tie them to your leader and you're ready to fish. The ubiquitous *clinch* or *improved clinch knots* will do in a pinch, but the salmon hook's distinctive upturned eye makes other knots more effective. A wet fly swims more smoothly and convincingly with a proper salmon fly knot.

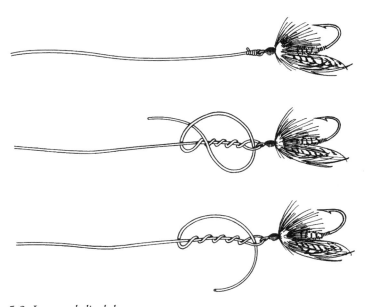

Figure 5-2. Improved clinch knot

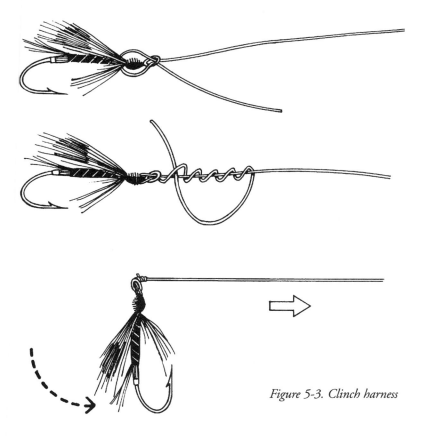

Figure 5-3. Clinch harness

The *turtle knot*—the classic salmon knot—is essentially a small harness that fits nicely around the hook eye, with the leader protruding at the desired angle. But the *clinch harness* (see fig. 5-3) is much simpler and generally stronger, and achieves the same result. I now use this exclusively. The key to tying this knot successfully is to hold the fly at a right angle to the leader as you draw the moistened knot down tightly, seating the harness at the base of the eye. If you just pull the leader tight, with the fly and leader in line, the harness will seat at the front of the eye.

The clinch knot is used with dry flies. Although the standard kind works fine with thicker leaders, make sure you use the improved clinch knot with leaders of fine diameter.

CHAPTER 6

On the River

Salmon fishing is a lot like looking for that Rolex watch one of the bigwigs lost during his brief appearance at the company picnic. First you need to narrow the search and determine where to begin; there's no point in searching the softball field if he didn't go there, and you needn't bother to crawl through the poison ivy. With the most likely area in mind, you need to comb every square foot of turf thoroughly and quasi-scientifically, not because finding a watch is a scientific act, but precisely because it isn't. That's why you conduct the search in a rational, organized way. Finally you need to pay constant attention; you don't want to walk right by the darned thing.

The chief component in successful salmon fishing is rivercraft: identifying and understanding the different types of water that hold salmon, and maximizing your awareness of what is—or isn't—happening there. Learning to use your eyes effectively is probably the most underestimated aspect of successful salmon fishing. The salmon's itinerant nature and marked preference for certain areas of rivers often makes fishing for it more like hunting than like most other kinds of fly fishing. Once you understand this, fishing for salmon becomes like combing the grass for a lost watch. Mostly it takes patience. Sometimes it doesn't even require that.

So there you are, on the bank of a river you've never fished, wondering where to begin. If you're lucky enough to be fishing with a guide from a private or commercial camp, most of your problems are solved (more on fishing with guides later in this chapter). But if you're fishing solo on public water, even some of the great water with limited public access, you have some important decisions to make. In most cases you can bring a certain amount of valuable information to this decision-making process in advance.

Salmon fishing is a highly regulated enterprise, and you can gather a lot of hard information before leaving for salmon country. Forget about finding great undiscovered or overlooked salmon fisheries in the United States or Canada; there aren't any. The fish is so highly prized and pursued that private angling organizations as well as federal and provincial agencies closely monitor the annual run as well as the annual exploitation of the resource. Thus for many rivers catch statistics (see appendix II) are available, as are statistics for the number of *rod days*.

Rod days are a good but tricky measure of both usage and productivity. A river posting 62 rod days in the month of July wasn't necessarily fished by 62 different anglers nor, obviously, for 62 days in one month. Those 62 days may represent the efforts of only seven anglers—five who fished for 12 consecutive days beginning July 1 and two who fished on the last day of the month, with not a soul fishing between July 13 and July 31.

Or those 62 rod days may represent 31 different anglers, each fishing for two days. Or maybe 62 anglers showed up on July 4, fished for the day, and departed, leaving the river unfished for the rest of the month. I use these extreme, unrealistic examples to show how rod days alone aren't a reliable indicator of how many anglers you can expect to encounter on your trip.

The *angler success ratio,* arrived at by dividing the number of rod days by the number of fish caught, is also a handy statistic. A 0.5 success rate means that, on average, one salmon is caught for every two rod days. But remember, this does *not* mean that every angler who fished the river for two days caught a fish. On public water, a small number of effective anglers almost always account for a disproportionately large number of fish. And most of these fish are caught in a relatively brief period (or periods) when angling conditions are ideal.

Some rivers (including the Matane) have fish counters installed at a downstream point of passage, so that you can find out on any given day how many fish have entered the river to date and when the bulk of them arrived. Most fisheries have either provincial or ZEC offices right on the river, where you can get updates on water and weather conditions as well as the number of rods on the river. The offices also keep log books for recording each fish caught along with the name of the pool where it was taken.

It's safe to assume that many fish go unreported, either from sheer angler laziness or secretiveness. On heavily fished water, even the most conscientious anglers are loathe to divulge where they caught their fish. This explains why every salmon angled on the Matapedia's public water for the last 15 years, including mine, was caught in the Salmon Hole.

The regulatory offices also provide free river maps of most public rivers, with all pools named and numbered. These maps are a great asset, at least for navigational purposes. They don't indicate a pool's productivity or when it's likely to contain salmon, however. And they aren't updated often enough to incorporate important riverbed or riparian changes. But asking a few questions, with map in hand, will help you understand these things.

Given the unreliability of log books, the best indicator of pool quality comes from asking provincial or ZEC personnel and other anglers which pools are the most heavily fished. Mark those pools on your map, draw some conclusions, then devise a plan, even if your fishing partner thinks it's a cockamamy one. For instance, you may decide to start each morning by fishing the first pool below one of the best pools (unless, of course, one of the best pools is unoccupied), on the theory that you might be early enough to intercept fish before they move into a prime pool to rest for the day.

Perhaps a map shows the river bending away from the road for a good distance, with only two named pools in the entire stretch. Unless one or both of them happen to be first-rate pools, most anglers probably won't bother making the long walk to fish them—not when it means losing expensive fishing time. If the water below and between the pools is rough, very shallow, or slow (something you can learn by asking), there's a fair chance that fish will rest at least briefly in those two pools.

For a variety of reasons I prefer to fish the heavily pounded pools on public rivers only during "off" hours—at midday—or if I have a specific goal, such as trying a dry fly over a visible fish; or sometimes I'll take a quick pass through the very head or tail of a pool, which a lot of anglers miss in their haste to hit the hot spot(s). I've caught most of my fish in secondary pools (which I'll describe below), overlooked parts of popular pools, and undefined stretches of water where traveling salmon took up temporary lies. I caught those fish because I spent a lot of time looking for them instead of pounding away at a marquee pool containing nine other anglers—and no salmon.

In fact the first salmon I ever saw angled was a huge cockfish taken at midday while it moved through the shallow tail of a pool on the Ste. Anne River. Richard Franklin and I—a couple of kids steeped in the sport's rigid, traditional lore but without any actual experience in it— found the whole experience most instructive. We were on our way to pick up new permits after a morning spent fishing in the traditional way. As we jounced along the rough dirt road above the river, we saw a local angler and a guide engaged in a mighty struggle on the riverbank 20 yards below.

We pulled over and watched as the two men dragged a 35-pound salmon up through the bushes and onto the dirt road. The fish was bleeding profusely from the gills, and the guide was smeared with blood. As we watched, this rough-looking fireplug of a man cut off the magnif- icent salmon's quarter-size adipose fin, threw it in the road, recited a French curse, and spat. Apparently we were witnessing some kind of ritual—one very different from the elegant, graceful rites that had drawn us to salmon fishing.

The fly, still lodged in the salmon's jaw, was a trout-size Muddler Minnow trailing from a cheap fiberglass rod fitted with a tinny reel. I was still trying to digest this visceral tableau when the lucky angler began shouting and waving his arms at his companion, fishing on the far side of the river. Another salmon of the same size was slowly swimming toward the man, who obviously didn't see it. For a few moments I thought—even hoped—that it might bite off the guy's leg, but the fish eventually turned toward deeper water and vanished.

So while a river map can tell you many things, suggest an angling strategy, and get you off to a good start, always remember that fish may be encountered anywhere. The rest of salmon fishing is rivercraft, which begins with understanding the three types of pools that exist on typical salmon rivers: primary, secondary, and tertiary.

READING A RIVER

Primary pools always contain fish, often in great numbers. Primary pools are often *holding pools,* where fish may sometimes remain for weeks on end. This kind of ideal habitat may occur in only five or six places along an entire river, almost always in its middle or upper reaches.

Most primary pools have great character and definition, because they're usually born of the clash between an unstoppable natural force (water) and an immovable object (the base of a mountain or a formation of granite) that meet under rugged conditions (a sharp drop in elevation) and force the river into a dramatic configuration.

The typical primary pool usually begins where a drop in elevation creates a strong, fast riffle or run that is forced to turn. Over the years the volume and speed of water flowing through this tight turn gouges out a deep hole on the inside of the turn, creating a trough that becomes a depository for geological detritus, including the large stones that create great salmon lies. As the pool broadens on its way downstream, the water slows and collects in a deep reservoir. Gradually the pool again becomes shallow, and the water begins to pick up speed near the tailout. Often the tailout's combination of bottom rubble and glassy, smooth flow creates additional resting lies just above the break, where the pool ends and another riffle begins.

The most common characteristic of a primary pool is depth, and the sign of a holding pool is enough depth to create a reservoir—the equivalent of an enormous fish tank—in which the salmon wait until another rise of water or the urgency of the impending spawning season encourages them to move along. The sure sign of a holding pool is the sight of salmon suspended in nearly still, deep water. Such fish are usually in holding mode and very tough to catch. But the same pool may also contain salmon in stationary positions in the swifter water near its head or tail, and these fish are more likely to take a fly.

Primary pools that don't serve as holding pools usually lack a reservoir. Some are just too far downriver to hold fish for long. Others can't satisfy the salmon's need for good depth and cold water as the summer progresses.

Some of the best primary pools are created where large tributaries, particularly those used for spawning, enter a river. Although the stretch may look bland, there's always a significant change in depth and a variation in flow where a tributary enters a river, and the volume of water pushed into the river during high water always creates a pool. A big tributary presents salmon with a fork in the road, and the fish react predictably: They stop to decide which way to go. As the season progresses they often stop for a long time, because of the refreshing, cool water flowing in from the trib.

Secondary pools often hold fish, but rarely in great numbers or for long periods. The typical secondary pool is a place where, even during peak water levels, the river just doesn't have enough force, or doesn't meet enough riparian resistance, to carve and gouge out the dramatic aquatecture typical of holding pools.

A secondary pool often begins with a decline in elevation and a riffle as well, but there may be no natural obstruction to force the river to turn and dig out a deep hole. In such places the sheer force of water rushing through the riffle will create some scouring at the point where the terrain levels off; the water suddenly gets slower and deeper, forming a pool. In other places the bank on the outside of a turn may be overwhelmed by high water, with the river eventually overrunning it and creating an island; a secondary pool may form below the island at the convergence of the two swift riffles flanking it.

On any given salmon river, the majority of pools are secondary. There's great variety among them, and they often must be fished differently. In primary pools the best fishing is usually at the very top and bottom. In secondary pools, the middle section often fishes best, because that's where the water has attained sufficient depth without having slowed too much.

Tertiary pools sometimes hold fish, usually depending on water level. A tertiary pool is often a part-time pool—a *high-water pool,* or a *low-water pool.* Under ideal conditions, a tertiary pool can be as hot as any other. Except for the high-water types, tertiary pools are usually small.

There are two kinds of high-water pools. One is created in areas where the water moves too slowly most of the time to hold fish. These places usually aren't pools in the traditional sense, but specific places with good structure and reasonable depth in sluggish stretches of river. They can be difficult to identify. The other kind of high-water pool is a more conventional pool that's just too shallow under medium to low flows to attract salmon.

Tertiary pools often are formed where small tributaries enter rivers, or by a particular riparian feature, such as a stone formation jutting out from the bank in a straight stretch of river. In either case, high water may gouge out enough of the streambed to create a change of depth, a better variety of bottom structure, or both. In many cases high water creates a distinct, temporary current or seam of swifter water. Fish may rest in such places temporarily under all water conditions, but they're usually angled best during high water.

Runs don't fit easily into any of the previous categories, even though they're often either parts of pools or identified as pools on river maps for the sake of convenience. A run is a relatively deep stretch of river that rolls along at a good clip. My definition of a run (as opposed to a *riffle*) is simple: If I can't see what's lying on the bottom, it's a run.

You can find runs where the topography forces a river into a narrow channel, where a river runs tight against the base of a mountain, or alongside a riprapped bank. Some of the most productive runs are right below heavily fished primary pools, where all the pool's outgoing water is forced to pass briskly through a narrow gap in the tailout. This funneling effect, combined with topographical features, often directs a large volume of water downstream through a narrow, deep channel.

One of the best examples of a run is the productive "choke" below Salmon Hole on the Matapedia. Runs like these are difficult to read, and you have to fish them thoroughly and patiently. They may hold fish at any given time.

By virtue of location, some secondary pools become primary ones. Usually this occurs where a secondary pool is the only pool of any kind at the upstream end of a very long rough or shallow stretch of river. It often seems that the farther salmon have to travel through unappealing water, the more likely they are to rest at the first pool they enter; closely spaced pools seem to encourage fish to move quickly rather than slowly. There may be various reasons for this, but fatigue isn't one of them. Always remember that under all but the most adverse circumstances, salmon can move upriver as quickly—or slowly—as they please.

Spots are small, attractive areas in the midst of otherwise fallow water. I've done a fair amount of spot fishing with surprisingly good results. Typical spots include a group of larger rocks lying in a slight depression in a broad, shallow stretch of river; the area around a single large boulder where the river has good depth and flow but a uniform bottom of small river stones; and a waist-deep flat area in the middle of a long stretch of whitewater. You find spots by stumbling onto them while looking for fish; even when you can't see whether fish are in them, you can cover them with a dozen or so casts.

Of course, specific river characteristics can change the relative importance of different types of riverine structure. The Matapedia, for instance, is an "old" river flowing through a broad valley with a relatively even grade. Many of its best areas are actually runs, and some of its most productive pools have secondary characteristics. By contrast the nearby Matane flows through rugged country that creates a remarkable pool-per-mile ratio, and the dramatic landscape gives many of the Matane's pools primary characteristics. One of the reasons I enjoy fishing the Matane is that the sheer number of pools there means I can often find privacy without sacrificing my confidence in the quality of water I'm fishing.

A POOL IN DETAIL

Let's zero in on one specific pool to see the different types of water and fishing situations that it offers, and where we can find salmon under different water conditions. Let's make this a real pool, one that I know well: the Home Pool of Maclennan Lodge on the Upsalquitch River (see fig. 6-1).

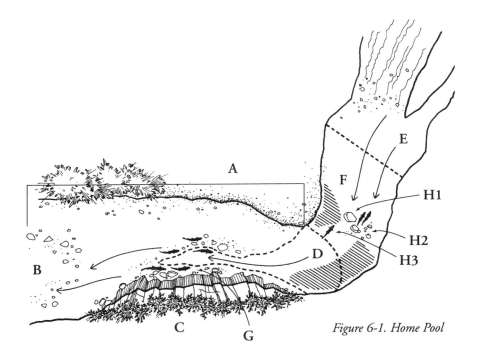

Figure 6-1. Home Pool

Home Pool is a primary pool, although it isn't a classic holding pool. The Upsalquitch flows south to north and so has a west and an east bank. For convenience I'll refer to these banks and other features as either left or right, always assuming we're facing downstream, as we usually do when salmon fishing.

Home Pool begins at the lower end of a long, brisk run that deepens quickly as it comes up against a steep slope, forcing the river to turn right and creating a deep hole and a large eddy on the inside of the turn. For about the next 200 yards the river runs straight along the base of the slope, which is really a long shoulder of granite; the left bank is a nearly vertical wall of pine clinging to mossy ledgerock.

In the upper portion of this stretch ledgerock and granite formations shelve out into the river, some extending all the way out to the main channel, where they drop off like miniature underwater cliffs. We call this entire area of the left bank the Ledges. The main channel is distinct and littered with colored gravel, rocks, and boulders of varying sizes. It follows the rough, occasionally broken line of ledgerock, gradually becoming less pronounced until both features dissolve into the beginning of a broad, shallow tailout carpeted with small stones.

From the riffle above the turn, the entire right bank is a beach of small stones that slopes into the river—steeply at the eddy created by the deep hole and very gradually down near the tail of the pool, where the shore is flat and brushy.

Under ideal, medium-water conditions, we usually fish about 75 yards of the run above the pool itself, so we're talking about fishing a 275-yard-long pool on a river that during average flow is about 40 yards wide. This sounds like a lot of water. It *is* a lot of water, until you begin to identify the *taking water* where a fish is likely to grab a fly.

There are *dead zones,* which we don't bother to fish at all, for the following reasons:

Zone A: The water on the inside of the turn and below has insufficient current; in fact, the entire right bank is just a dumping ground for the small stones that annually get pushed and washed down the river on high water. This is such a powerful—but smooth—natural event that it has created a beautiful beach along the entire bank.

Zone B: The tailout of Home Pool is very broad and shallow, with neither a sufficient flow nor structure to attract fish that have come up from the riffle below. Home Pool fish head right for the middle of the pool.

Zone C: The riverbed along the left bank here is flat, smooth ledgerock. We've never seen a fish here.

Zone D: The heart of Home Pool is about 15 feet deep. It doesn't have enough current to fish a wet fly well, and the dry fly is only slightly more effective in water of such depth. However, we do work on fish we happen to see here, and guide Shane Mann and I once took a 24-pound salmon in the upper portion of the deep hole on a green and yellow Bomber.

Suddenly, Home Pool has become a lot smaller. Now let's identify a place where we sometimes fish, but rarely with any success:

Zone E: The upper part of the run is relatively shallow, swift, and generally even-bottomed. Sometimes we take a grilse there (grilse seem comfortable holding in surprisingly swift and shallow water), but that's about it. However, the run fishes pretty well during high water, especially in the extreme upper portion, which has a name of its own: Plum Beach.

Now you should have a much more realistic picture of this fine pool; the water we fish with confidence represents just a fraction of it. Even that fraction can be divided into two very different areas, which we approach very differently.

Zone F: This run is all good taking water, with enough depth and variety in the bottom structure to hold salmon and grilse. But the hot spots are the two large rocks near the very bottom of the riffle (H-1) and the smaller rocks just to the left of them (H-2). The other excellent area here is the very bottom of the run on the right (H-3), where the water is swift but a little slower and deeper. Although this is ideal wet-fly water, we often switch to dry flies when a fish shows interest, or if we want to probe around the rocks.

Zone G: Almost all the fish caught in the body of Home Pool are taken out of this trough, which is no wider than 10 yards at any point, between 3 and 5 feet deep, and clearly defined between the ledgerock on the left and a bottom of small, smooth stones on the right. The abundance of structure in the channel encourages fish to take up lies almost anywhere (see fig. 6-2). The pool's even flow and holding capacity ensure that it fishes well through most water conditions, with the taking areas expanding and contracting as the water rises or ebbs.

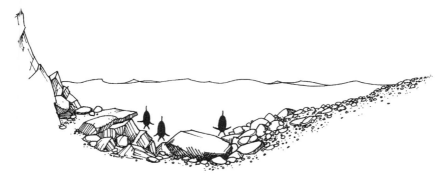

Figure 6-2. Cross-section of Zone G of Home Pool.

Now let's look at the small picture: a typical area that holds salmon based on the main channel in Zone G of Home Pool (see figs. 6-2 and 6-3). The gradient of the channel from one side to the other is gentle on the right and steep on the left (see fig. 6-2). This holding area has three important areas distinguished by three aquatectural features: a long, rectangular boulder (Lie 1), an underwater bluff (Lies 2 and 3), and a tablerock (Lie 4).

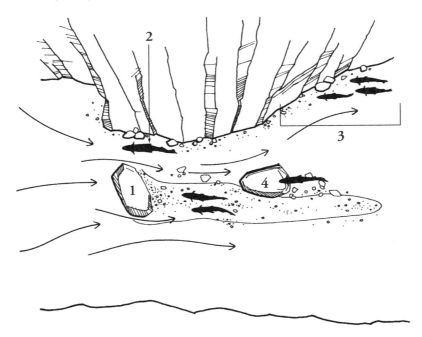

Figure 6-3. Overview of Zone G of Home Pool.

The boulder is in the middle of the main channel. It has practically sheer faces and is thickest at its upstream end, where its rough top creates some turbulence on the river's otherwise glassine surface.

The underwater bluff is part of a massive formation of ledgerock jutting straight out into the channel from the left bank. The tip of this bluff is 3 feet tall, but as the formation extends downstream, heading back toward the shore at about a 30-degree angle, it tapers to just a few inches. It's surrounded by rubble on the bottom.

The tablerock slopes up out of the river bottom at a gentle angle, so that its downstream end is only about 10 inches above the gravel. The tablerock is well below the boulder and across from the middle of the bluff.

Figure 6-3 shows that seven salmon are holding in this area at medium water level, in four distinct lies.

- One fish lies in the deep water just off and behind the point of the bluff.
- Three grilse rest amid the rubble in the glide at the downstream end of the formation.
- One fish rests with its chin just a few inches above the middle of the downstream end of the flat rock.
- Two salmon hold comfortably in the mild, gravelly depression created by years of scouring behind the boulder.

So why there?

Although this is a theoretical scenario, rivercraft suggests the following: The solitary large salmon in Lie 2 has enough bulk to hold comfortably in the strong current washing around and along the wall of the bluff. The fish amid the rubble in Lie 3, an unexpectedly attractive place, are in a mere 2 feet of water but not outside the influence of structure. The water is slightly deeper inside the bluffline, and the current channeled through there meets the flow gently flooding over from the shallows along the left bank in a way that is particularly attractive to grilse—which are more likely than salmon to adopt "flow" lies.

Lie 4 provides a specific, small zone of comfort for the fish. Here, under identical water conditions, you'll see different fish over the years with their chins in almost exactly the same place, as if the water between the back edge of the rock and the fish were a cushion. Clearly, salmon like the way the water flows over this natural stone ramp.

The two salmon like Lie 1 because it offers relief from two conflicting currents, one created by the bluff and one by the rectangular boulder. But the lie is far enough below the boulder to have a consistent flow of its own. Annual scouring creates a "saucer" in which these fish lie, near rubble deposited on the margin of the main current during high water.

High-water conditions create more holding areas, and fish tend to spread out. Even when specific lies are eliminated by fast flows, larger, suitable resting areas offering more lies are created. In our model, increased current speed wipes out the special velocity-dependent appeal of Lies 1 and 4. A combination of water speed and the increased conflict between different currents makes Lie 2 too turbulent. And as figure 6-4 shows, high water significantly alters the viability of Lie 3. A new Lie, 5, where a number of fish hold, is created farther back along the bluff but in the main channel. And the rubble along the slope of the channel, with its even, moderate current, creates a new resting area—Lie 6—occupied by three fish.

Low water shrinks holding areas and eliminates lies (see fig. 6-5). With a less vigorous flow and more of the boulder diverting the current

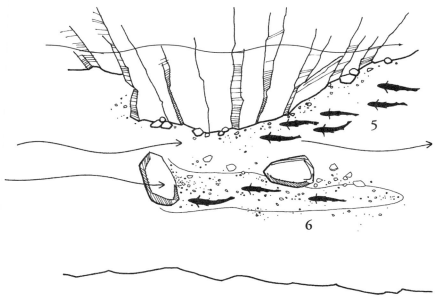

Figure 6-4. High-water lie

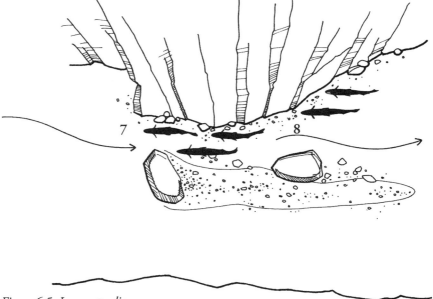

Figure 6-5. Low-water lie

toward midchannel, a new Lie, 7, is established up off the point of the boulder; it overlaps with the new Lie 8. The bluff becomes the primary source of comfort for the fish, providing valuable shade along with a place to rest. All the desirable lies on the right side of the channel are wiped out by low water.

The important thing to remember about this scenario is that the pool offers fish the best variety of resting habitat at moderate water levels. Under high-water conditions the fish could be almost anywhere in the main channel, while during low-water periods they have to be in a single place.

Shane Mann and I fish Home Pool from a canoe and explaining how we do so will be useful to consider. We take the canoe from the landing at the very tail of Home Pool and motor very slowly up along the right bank. Shane usually stands on his seat in the stern, steering and working the small outboard's throttle with his right foot (don't try this at home, folks), while we both look for fish in Zone G.

We motor all the way up to the deep hole then work our way back down. We anchor across and slightly up from any fish we've seen (preferably at least 40 feet away) and go to work on them. Most of the time we use dry flies. There have been days when Shane counted up to 30 salmon in the pool and was unable to raise one. At other times, the only two fish he saw in the pool took a fly. On the rare occasions when there are no salmon in the channel, or after we have caught or quit on them, we motor up and fish the run in Zone F.

So the canoe is a tremendous luxury that not only makes it easier to fish Home Pool, but also saves us enormous amounts of time. It has allowed me to know this pool intimately. Over the years we've been able

Restigouche fishing canoes (Photo: Val Atkinson)

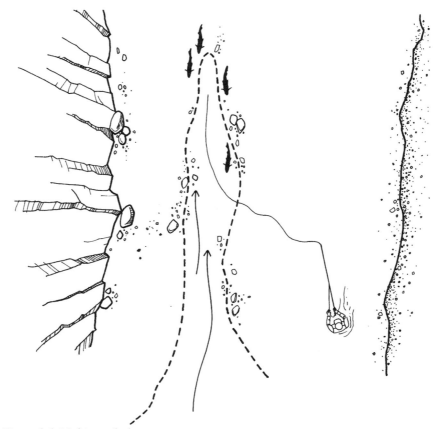

Figure 6-6. Making a slack-water presentation

to observe the habits and reactions of Home Pool's salmon in what amounts to de facto lab conditions.

Now consider the problems you would face even as an experienced wading angler trying Home Pool for the first time (refer to fig. 6-1). You'd know enough to fish from the right bank, starting up in the run, but not enough to concentrate on Zone F. Because of your low vantage point while wading, you probably wouldn't make out the dark shape of the rocks at H-1 and H-2.

Fishing in the traditional down-and-across style (which I'll discuss in chapter 7), you may be unable to cover hot spots H-1 and H-2 even if you do know about them. It would take a superhuman cast to reach the rocks at H-2, and it would be hard to get a good swing over the two large rocks at H-1. However, you would be in an excellent position to show a fly to any fish in area H-3.

In most of Zone A, the water depth would prevent you from wading out far enough to make the long cast necessary to cover the upper portion of Zone G properly. You'd have to settle for the lower two-thirds of Zone G, with a really good swing possible only in the lower half of the zone. Furthermore, the slack water in front of you would pose thorny presentation problems. After any given cast, the front half of your line would be swept along by the current, while the half closer to you would just lie there (see fig. 6-6). The good news is that the bottom half of Zone G is an excellent spot.

You can see, then, that the wading angler's chances are reduced by simple logistics, never mind any other factors. The point I'm trying to make is not about the superiority of boat fishing but about the wader's need to understand his situation and then do everything he can to improve his chances. That's where scouting comes into play.

Don't ever just run down to a pool and begin fishing, armed only with the noble—and generally correct—idea that the harder and longer you fish, the better will be your chances. No matter how long and hard you fish over barren water or a dead zone in otherwise good water, your chances will still be zero. Make every effort to understand a pool prior to fishing, preferably at an off time such as midday. And make full use of your best tool, your eyes.

Over the years I've spent about as much time scouting as I have fishing. This is true in the specific sense of scouting pools prior to fishing as well as the general sense of spending a lot of time wandering the riverbank, looking for salmon.

Most high banks—whether a railroad track, a road's shoulder, or the top of a rock slide—offer good viewing points. Climbing trees can be equally helpful, as can the age-old pastime of people with a little too much time on their hands: standing on a bridge and staring into the water. Although it can be difficult to measure water speed or even depth from such vantage points, they are great aids in identifying the taking water in pools and the best place from which to fish them.

Let's say that Home Pool is on a public stretch of water paralleled by a two-lane blacktop. If you pulled over to check out the pool from above, you'd notice the rocks at H-1 and H-2 (refer to fig. 6-1). The adventurous angler might try to figure out a way to cover those areas from the left bank, contrary to the conventional logic revealed by the footpaths of previous anglers. The water near the left bank in Zones E and F is shallow and slow moving, because the thrust of the run comes from the right bank, so you could cover the rocks very nicely from the left bank.

I also mentioned that the left bank in Zones C and D (refer to fig. 6-1) is steep and rough. If you hacked your way through the brush, you'd find one or more excellent places from which to analyze the pool from above. You'd see things that a wader couldn't and thereby quickly realize the need to concentrate your efforts on the relatively small area of the channel. And you might make a note to cover the upper part of the channel in the only way possible: with a dry fly fished across stream and dropped no farther than the *near* side of the underwater ledges.

In Home Pool, seeing fish from the high left bank would be difficult because they often lie close to, or in the shadow of, the ledges. But other bank and pool configurations are conducive to spotting fish. Casting over water known to contain a fish, especially if you can *see* it, brings a little more spice to angling and is a wonderful tonic for boredom, to which even the most stoic angler may succumb after a few days of unsuccessful blind fishing.

SEEING FISH

Learning to see fish is easy: Just stare into the water for a good part of every day, every summer, for about 20 years. That's how David and Shane Mann learned to do it, and I'm not sure there is any other way. I thought I had pretty good eyes for fish until I met the Manns. Often Shane points out fish and *even then* I can't see them, although I have become pretty good at pretending I do, then figuring out where to cast by asking a few subtle questions.

You can learn to spot fish more readily if you keep some things in mind. Salmon look much smaller than you'd expect, and the deeper the water, the smaller they look. In rolling water, it's practically impossible to see grilse. If you're good you might spot one salmon in such water—but miss three others. Most important, you can rarely see into rolling water well enough to make the most valuable of all judgments: that the run or pool contains *no* fish.

The best places to spot salmon are in tailouts, glides, and main channels relatively free from surface turbulence. To reduce distortion and glare, wear a hat with a brim, try to look as straight down into the water as possible, and cup your hands around the sides of your polarized sunglasses. Gray or brown lenses are the most popular on bright days, but I use the yellow lenses recommended for low-light conditions almost exclusively. They have great light-gathering ability.

I know this will smack of Zen mumbo-jumbo, but it's really true: Don't look too fiercely for a fish; allow it to reveal itself to you. Look *through* the water instead of *at* it. Take in a whole area at a time instead of focusing on a sequence of specific objects. You won't find fish with your peripheral vision (unless they suddenly move into it, but then moving fish are always easier to see); still, allowing your attention to flood toward the peripheral is a fine way to rest your eyes, making them more effective when you next need to focus.

Obviously water clarity has a lot to do with visibility, but almost all Canadian salmon rivers have good to excellent clarity. The real key to good visibility is bottom composition. Riverbeds composed mostly of light or pale stones and gravel have two critical advantages: They reflect a lot more light, and they provide a lot more contrast.

When you begin actively searching the river, you'll be amazed at how many river rocks actually look like fish. Although I've yet to see a rock shaped anything like a salmon, the interplay of stone, light, and shadow has tremendous illusory effects. When you really want to see a salmon, you can convince yourself that almost anything with a front and back end is one. But there are a few ways to eliminate most of those granite fish.

Although color varies by individual fish and by how long a salmon has been in the river, fresh fish almost always look smoke gray in the water. Granted, most rivers have a lot of gray rocks, but you can at least eliminate the brown, yellow, and mossy green ones.

A fish in a resting lie always faces directly upstream. It's surprising how few rocks that resemble fish are actually positioned correctly relative to the current. Perhaps it's the odd angles at which so many rocks rest in the water that make them look like fish. This is one of those weird things you'll notice only if you think about it—a trick played by optical phenomena such as distortion and foreshortening, with generous help from your eager imagination. Focusing on a suspected fish's angle to the current is the best way to break down and reveal the illusion before your mind gets too carried away.

If you still think you see a fish, look for a shadow on the bottom beneath it. In almost all smooth-water salmon lies, the fish are far enough off the bottom to cast a black shadow that's sometimes more conspicuous than the fish itself. Now look for a tail. Is it at the correct end of the alleged salmon? Is it moving? Unlike rocks, all salmon have tails that fan gently, even at rest. Tails are usually a bit lighter and greener than the fish's body.

Now proceed to the other end of your salmon, known as the front, or head. Can you see the white inside of the mouth? I'm not kidding. Resting salmon often work their mouths in a way that's strikingly obvious from a significant distance. Don't throw your visible-fish theory out the window if you can't see the fish's mouth working, but do abandon it if the thing you have been staring at from up in that tree ends in a right angle.

Staring, by the way, is not a good thing when looking for fish. Stare at anything long enough and it will become whatever you want it to be. It will also appear to move, breathe, break-dance, whatever. Unless you have the discipline to absorb and evaluate a potential fish without staring at it, rest your eyes by turning away after a few seconds and briefly looking at something entirely different. The longer you hem and haw about an unknown object, the less likely it is to be a fish.

Losing and regaining sight of a potential fish in rolling water is often a good sign. A salmon has the same graceful shape as any creature designed to exist in the heavy medium of flowing water. Even the largest salmon may appear as slender as a wisp of smoke in the current, and become visible only under momentary flow conditions. I can't tell you how to look for something as vague and magical as life, but salmon express it as a hovering lightness.

Detecting a real salmon has similarities to a religious conversion. Something clicks, and from that moment on the object is so clearly and obviously a fish that you can never see it as a rock again, even if you try.

There is one other crucial dimension to scouting pools and looking for fish: orientation. This is the invaluable art of remembering where that hot spot was, or where the two salmon were lying, *after* you've walked back to the car, driven upstream, crossed the river, walked back, and suddenly seen the pool from a radically different angle. Things that seem so obvious from the high bank have a way of becoming confusing and even disappearing.

Whenever possible, mark in-stream locations by shoreline landmarks such as distinctly shaped or colored rocks, deadfalls, or odd trees. And make sure that their distinctive features will be visible from where you'll be fishing.

I'm always amazed at how difficult it is to judge the correct location of specific riverbed features, or even fish, from different angles. Let's say you're out scouting from a high bank and you see a salmon lying about 15 yards out from the far bank, just downstream of two large, pale yellow rocks. You quickly note the dead pine on the far bank, directly in line with the fish. The river is too swift to cross, so you'll have to fish from the near bank, wading out as far as you dare.

You walk 100 yards upstream to the steep path leading down to the river and make your way back downstream. Your heart beats faster as you pick out the dead pine, feeling confident that you have a good bead on the salmon. You enter the water far enough upstream to get a good swing over the fish and cautiously begin to wade out.

As you survey the situation from this new vantage, however, you grow unsure about your ability to pinpoint a spot 35 yards away, straight out from the pine tree on the far bank. The perspective is very flat, and you're not sure of the angle to the pine. You try to make out the yellow rocks that were so obvious from above, but from this angle the river's surface is opaque. Soon the water is swirling around your waist; this run is both deeper and swifter than it looked from above. You're still a long way off when you lose your footing on a mossy rock and almost fall in; you realize that wading farther out is unwise.

Deep down, you feel that this isn't going to work; you'll never be able to locate and cover the fish the way you had planned, the way that looked so easy from the high bank. In fact you look at the high bank and try to find the spot where you stood, but you can't. Now you're *really* confused.

You know what? That's fishing, even for veterans. That's why you should try to do all the little things that, even if you fail, will allow you at least to understand *why* you failed. In this case you could have marked your spotting position in addition to the target positions. The more points of reference you have, the better.

On any given day on the river, your eyes should work as much as your arms or legs. Watching your fly is so important that sometimes, during long fishless periods, I consciously look up into the sky and mutter a mantra about not even wanting to catch a salmon, on the highly suspect premise that this would be the ideal time for a fish as fickle as a salmon to whack my fly. It has never worked.

Salmon that make a pass at a fly often leave a huge boil or make a great splash as they turn away, but it's surprising how often the sign of interest is as subtle as a small spurt of water, created by the tip of the salmon's tail. Always watch for any irregularity in the water near your fly, no matter how minor.

For a variety of reasons, including human impatience, a taking salmon of which you're unaware may get only one decent look at a fly. (It should get at least three.) If you miss a signal of interest, you may fish right over the salmon without giving it a good reason to come back a second time. But if you pick up a swirl, a flash of silver, or an upwelling of water behind the fly, you can give the fish every reasonable opportunity to take a number of flies. Most of the time fish that make at least one pass at a fly are taking fish. This is almost universally true when they make that pass on the first decent swing of the fly.

FISHING WITH GUIDES

If you're new to salmon fishing, trust your guide completely unless he gives you a legitimate reason to lose confidence. Very few guides in salmon country are glib or salesmanlike, but they usually possess great rivercraft. And they have a very traditional definition of what they do. You have to know a little bit about salmon fishing history and customs to fully appreciate this.

For many years, the late Randolph Thomas was the head guide for the Kedgwick River Lodge, while his wife, Ada, was the head cook at Maclennan Lodge. Randolph liked to talk about his extensive experience as a guide and about some of the sports with whom he fished. One fellow, an angling banker from New York, would sit in the canoe and

A seasoned guide will provide invaluable advice on pools, fly selection, and fishing techniques to beginners and experienced anglers alike (Photo: Val Atkinson)

read a book while Randolph fished. Each time he caught a salmon, the sport gave Randolph $20.

Most guides don't really care how far you cast or how much you know about salmon fishing or flies. They mostly want you to listen and let them call the shots. It isn't because they have big egos (although some do). It's because that's their job description: The guide is supposed to get you fish. If it were the other way around, the guide would be paying you.

But since you're paying him, you are also ultimately the boss. The biggest mistake you can make, though, is letting the guide know this, particularly if you demand that he do something he knows is foolish. One guest at Tucker's camp insisted on telling the guides where to anchor the boat, then proceeded to fish in a way most kindly described as unorthodox. The guides never said a word to that sport, but they let Tucker, who cares about such things, know how they felt. It was one of the reasons that the sport was never invited back.

Still, an experienced angler often wants to call his own shots and has every right to do so. But it's best to let the guide know that this represents your predisposition rather than your lack of confidence in him. I've often driven Tucker's guides nuts with my experiments in fly selection, and once I even managed to get Shane so frustrated that he snapped at me. I was secretly proud of that moment, because I took it to mean that Shane felt he knew me well enough to let me know how he really felt—something that a stubborn riverman rarely does.

Remember: Even if a guide isn't up on the latest in high-modulus graphite, he almost always knows the river and the fish in a way that only his kind, born and bred on the river, can. This is the most important and useful information a salmon angler can possess.

Angler and guide must work as a team to successfully bring an Atlantic salmon to net (Photo: Val Atkinson)

CHAPTER 7

Fishing the Wet Fly

Salmon fishing must be the sport of choice in paradise, because under ideal conditions it falls just enough short of child's play to remain interesting. The basic wet-fly technique is the easiest—and potentially most tedious—of all the methods by which fly anglers pursue gamefish. Using a simple two-stroke downstream cast, the angler casts a fly repeatedly at a 45-degree angle to the current, allows it to swing down, and then does absolutely nothing when a salmon takes it. Even a rank beginner can do this.

But this world isn't paradise, and despite the best efforts of organizations such as the Atlantic Salmon Federation, the problems salmon anglers face have less to do with mastering techniques than with a relative scarcity of fish, intense competition among various user groups, and unpredictable water conditions, which are partly the result of habitat degradation brought about by human activity.

Under the conditions most anglers encounter, successful salmon angling is complex. Fishing the wet fly successfully means dealing with a range of water conditions, maximizing the time a fly moves in a way that salmon find appealing, and covering the greatest amount of taking water with the least amount of effort.

Granted, this may not evoke the image of a thoughtful, pipe-smoking fly fisher plying his craft, a backlit line swishing audibly through the air while a faithful black Lab sits patiently on the riverbank. In comparison, it may even seem a bit grim. I was originally attracted to this sport because I'd heard that salmon were difficult—"the fish of a thousand casts." So I went out and fished the wet fly in the traditional manner, often from dawn to dusk, with the conviction that patience and stamina were the keys to success. Often that thousandth cast came and went, and the only jerk was at the wrong end of the line.

I eventually discovered that it's a lot more effective—and considerably more fun—to fish well than merely to fish hard. Yes, every salmon angler must be willing to don the hair shirt once in a while, to cast and cast and cast a wet fly with no apparent reason to continue doing so. And to tell the truth, that kind of masochism does contain a certain satisfaction: We catch salmon the old-fashioned way—we *earn* them. But day in, day out, you'll get better results if you have a plan, look for shortcuts, and cultivate a willingness to experiment rather than a saintly capacity to endure frustration.

I could cover the basic wet-fly technique in just a few pages, then send you out to repeat the drill until you catch a fish or turn blue. But I won't. Instead we're going to spend a pleasant sunny morning fishing a pool with a wet fly. Then I'll elaborate on the important events that transpired.

ON MATALIK POOL

Matalik, a pool on the upper portion of the Matapedia's public sector, is a classic secondary pool (see fig. 7-1). It begins at the end of a long run of swift water flowing through relatively flat land, at a point where a brook joins the river from the right. Just below this brook is a steep, wooded bank.

The run hits this bank at a relatively mild angle, so it hasn't gouged out a deep, dramatic hole. Instead, Matalik is a long bend pool going right to left with an even, gradual grade that features good depth—about

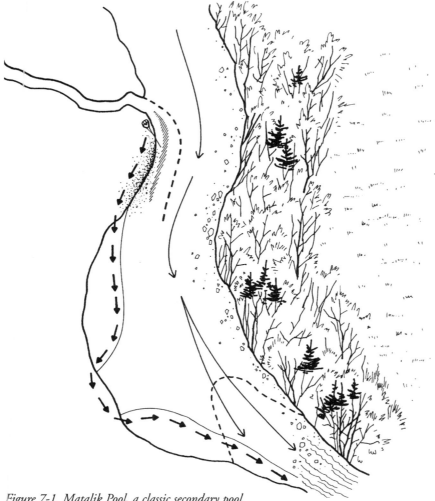

Figure 7-1. Matalik Pool, a classic secondary pool

8 feet at the inside of the turn, where the water is slowest. The end of the pool is broad and shallow, with a terrific, glassy tailout filled with large rocks near the left bank.

This pool is a quick study. The left bank is inaccessible from the road and overgrown right down to the water, with a large hayfield beyond the brush. All fishing is done from the right bank, which is also brushy to just above where the brook enters the river. It's obvious that the taking water begins at the mouth of the brook and extends for 60 yards along the gravel beach that begins just below the brook. Below that, the right bank is a narrow strip of dirt and rocks at the base of the wooded slope.

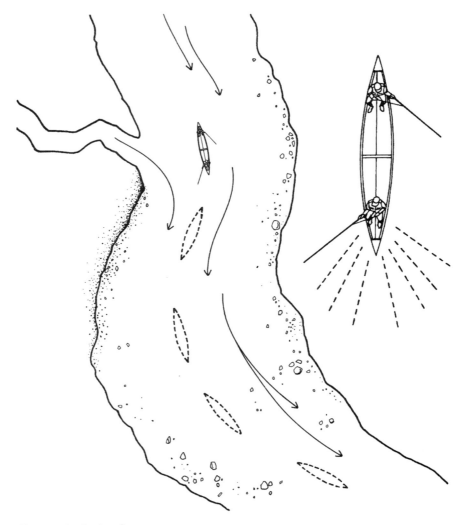

Figure 7-2. Casting from a canoe

Downstream of the bend, the water floods over to create a broad, shallow eddy on the right, while the left bank features that attractive tailout. All in all Matalik is a manageable 125 yards long, from the beginning of the taking water in the run to the whitewater and exposed rocks just below the tailout. The run is 25 yards wide, and the river spreads to about 35 yards at the heart of the pool. It's almost 50 yards wide at the bottom of the pool, including the large, shallow overflow area on the right. The tailout, through which most of the water passes, is only about 20 yards wide.

Anglers in a canoe would fish this pool in a succession of 50 foot drops, covering the water in the same methodical way as would a wading angler (see fig. 7-2). Anchoring midriver (in the main channel—refer to fig. 7-1) to fish each drop, the anglers would fish both sides of the boat, by alternating casts on either side or by fishing out one side at a time, thereby covering all the water. Fortunately boats spook salmon only in very shallow water; even then they generally just move away until the boat passes, then return to their lies. In fact salmon will often take a fly just a few feet from a boat.

As the anglers fish down, on each drop they'd gradually move closer to the left bank, because that's where the taking water is concentrated. They'd fish the tailout positioned very close to the left bank, covering all the water easily from the right side of the boat.

As a wading angler arriving at Matalik, you should first assess the pool. Make an educated guess about where the taking water begins and where it ends, and look for significant underwater structure or riparian features that might influence current speed and/or water depth. You have no choice but to fish this pool from the right bank. This means that as you proceed, your backcast will soon be into the high bank (I'm assuming you're right-handed), and this could present problems with brush or tree limbs.

Do you have a good two hours to fish Matalik carefully, or is your buddy coming back to pick you up in a half hour? In the latter case, you'd just try to hit a few of the more likely hot spots. If you hook a big salmon, what are your chances of landing it in this pool and this stretch of river (see chapter 9)?

The fly you fish will be suggested by the general conditions. Today the water is at a robust medium height. The run is swift and looks to be about 3 feet deep in the middle up by the brook, where you'll begin fishing. This could be a good place to find a grilse right off the bat. The morning is clear and sunny. A size 6 Green Machine, tied on a double hook, is an excellent choice and compatible with your leader—a 9-foot level length of stiff 12-pound-test mono that easily handles medium-size wet flies.

In a typical run you almost never wade out into the current to begin fishing. Instead you fish your way into it from a position very close to shore. This is especially true in Matalik, because the top of the taking water is clearly marked by the brook. Over the years the water entering from the brook has cut a mild trough in the riverbed. You can tell because immediately below the brook is a ribbon of slack, dark water about 5 feet wide between the edge of the gravel bar and the main current.

The area around the seam, where the slack water and current meet, is a potential hot spot, as is the trough. You can easily see that most of the water in the run comes down on the right, because the water near the left bank directly across from the brook is very fast, shallow, and even-bottomed. You're going to focus all your efforts on the deeper, right side of the river.

Take two or three steps out into the slack water, set your reel's drag just tight enough to prevent the spool from overrunning, and strip off line until the leader and 3 feet of line are out beyond the tiptop. Cast this short length of line down and across the river at an angle of about 45 degrees (see fig. 7-3) to the current, allowing the fly to swing around and

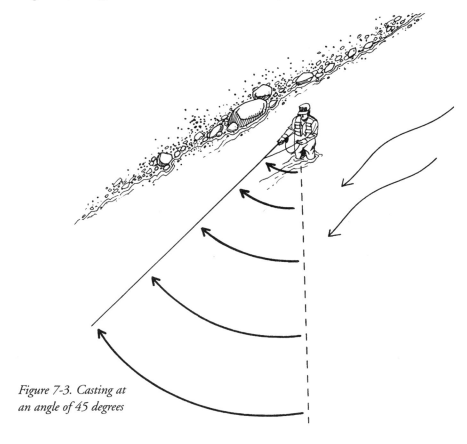

Figure 7-3. Casting at an angle of 45 degrees

straighten out below you. Keep your rod tip low, point it at the fly, and follow the fly through the swing. Hold the line coming off the reel loosely between the index and middle fingers of your right hand.

With 9 feet of rod and 12 feet of line and leader, even this short first cast covers a portion of the main channel and ultimately gets washed across it, into the slack water immediately below you. Now strip off about 2 feet of line, pick the line up off the water sharply, and shoot the new length downstream at the same 45-degree angle. The line lands straight and immediately the Green Machine begins to sweep across the water, just below the surface.

With so little line out, you can actually watch the fly's progress. Even though the current is swift, the fly moves slowly, looking like a gaudy, living creature trying to make headway against the current. This is the perfect swing—the most effective way to catch salmon.

At the end of the swing, strip off and hold another 2 feet of line, then repeat the cast. You can't see the fly now, but the taut line moving slowly across the current tells you the fly is doing exactly what it did on the last swing, only slightly downstream of its previous path. Repeat this process, still without moving from your spot: strip, backcast, forward cast, swing. Soon you settle into the cadence, feeling warm and relaxed. Life is good, and you constantly watch the general area of your fly.

Suddenly your rod tip begins to dance and you're barely able to restrain yourself from striking. You've hooked something—but it's tiny. Strip your line in by hand instead of reeling up, because you don't want to lose track of the length you were fishing. Bring the little fish in gently. It's as beautiful as a brook trout, but colored differently: a dark olive back; a pale, creamy belly; green and gold sides marked with seven dark, vertical, parallel bars with a single bright orange dot between each. The symmetry is astonishing.

This is a *parr*, a juvenile salmon too young to go to sea, and you'll catch quite a few most days on the river. That this beautiful miniature salmon has attacked a Green Machine half its size says a lot about the Atlantic salmon's bold, predatory nature. Treat it gently; you'd love for it to take your fly again three years down the road. Hold the body of the fly with the eye down and close to the water, and let the little parr wriggle free from the hook. It lands in the river with a splash and is instantly gone.

With about 30 feet of fly line out, you feel a pleasant, firm connection to the river. The steady tug of the water on your line puts a bit of a bend in your rod, and you can almost feel the little fly working against the current. You cast again, the line shoots out and lands dead straight, and the Green Machine begins to swim.

Soon you're casting 40-plus feet of line and getting an excellent drift over all the taking water in the run. With about 50 feet of line out, you reach the limit of your casting comfort zone—the amount of line you can cast repeatedly without straining your skill. In fact you've stumbled onto the *45-at-45 rule:* An ideal wet-fly cast is 45 feet long at a 45-degree angle to the current. There's no reason to push your cast, because up here in the pool's neck you're covering all the taking water with *this* one. From now on you'll cover new water by taking a moderate step downstream instead of by stripping off more line at the end of each cast.

You step and cast like this four or five times and then, at the very end of a drift, you're startled by a sharp pluck on the line. At the same time you see—or think you see—a spurt of water in the vicinity of your fly. You're not sure, though. It all happened so fast, and you were, well, unprepared.

When everything happens as it should in the classic wet-fly take, a salmon elevates from its lie, seizes the fly with confidence, then turns to go back to its place. Simultaneously you see a surface disturbance and feel a long, steady tug that often takes line right off your reel. You wait about three seconds (the British like to mutter "God Save the Queen") then briskly raise the rod to set the hook.

But it doesn't always happen this way. Sometimes fish slash at a fly and miss it, playfully nip at it, bump it, or chase it without ever taking it. The variations are endless, but they're generically known as *short takes.* There are days when the salmon will do everything *but* take a fly. Getting a salmon to show interest in a fly without actually taking it is called *rolling a fish.* The term also broadly describes a salmon that jumps or otherwise shows itself, as in "There were fish rolling all over the pool, but we couldn't get one to take."

If you roll a fish without hooking it, there's often a good chance that it will come back and take with greater commitment. But this time you aren't sure it was a salmon. The rap on your line was too sharp to have come from a parr. Perhaps a big brook trout bumped your fly, or maybe that spurt of water was an illusion.

Nevertheless, in a situation like this always assume that you rolled a salmon and act accordingly. At worst you'll just waste a little time—and better that than wasting a good opportunity. After rolling a fish, experienced anglers always rest it. In less health-conscious times, the rule of thumb was to rest a fish for as long as it took to smoke a cigarette. You don't really need to wait that long, but you must give the fish time to return to its lie. Give it at least 30 seconds.

The best way to pass the time is to check your drag and knots, *without* changing the exact amount of line you have out; remind yourself to stay calm, and analyze what just happened. Although the suspected salmon nipped the fly *on the dangle* (directly below you), it's unlikely it was holding in such slack water. Instead it probably followed the Green Machine from a lie somewhere in the main current. You can't see the bottom of the run, so the fish could be anywhere out there.

Before you make this critical cast, shorten up your line a few inches. In this situation, many anglers will fish exactly the same length of line. Others, even experienced ones who ought to know better, are tempted to strip out a little more line. This is understandable; it seems logical to assume that the salmon struck short because it didn't get "enough" of the fly. But salmon that want a fly have no trouble grabbing it as firmly as they like—unless you happen to be lifting it off the water just as they attack.

Repeat the cast, and when the fly lands make sure the line is clear of the rod butt and the reel handle. Nothing happens. Now try two more casts with your original length of line. *Nada.* Try three more casts, stripping off 6 inches of line each time. Still nothing. It's time to change flies.

Reel up 2 feet of line, then strip in the rest by hand so you can put the next fly in the right place. You want to make sure this fish gets a good first look at the new fly. You can be pretty sure you'll cover the salmon if it's established in a lie. Your brief encounter is unlikely to have been with a traveling salmon, because at this water level, on a bright, sunny morning, the run offers a good resting place.

You think about fishing a Green Highlander but decide that it isn't sufficiently different in color from the Green Machine. It's a bright day—

bright day, bright fly—so a Silver Rat would be appropriate. But you have a hunch—it's no fun always doing everything by the book—and choose a Black and Blue, a size 8 double. Because you reeled up 2 feet of line, there's no danger of placing your next cast below the fish. Stripping off 6 inches of line after each, you make five casts, and then, just as the fly swings around, you see a swirl, right in the seam where the current goes slack.

You wait thirty seconds and then fish the same cast again with great expectations. Nothing. As you stare at the spot where you saw the swirl, you notice little surface inconsistencies—dimples and swirls, and more swirls. Maybe it's just the flow of the water playing tricks on you. You fish the same cast again, then two slightly longer ones, but there's no sign of the fish.

You wish you knew for sure if a salmon was out there. You decide to try one more fly—the Silver Rat after all. Once again you thoroughly cover the area where the fish seems to rest. While you're fishing, a salmon rolls down in the heart of the pool. You've been working this fish for more than 20 minutes, but you're not even sure it's really there. It's time to move on. But first you glance at the shore and mark your spot by noting a rock with a vein of quartz at the water's edge.

You go back to the Green Machine, shorten up by 6 feet, and fish through; it's always a good idea to give a fish a last look at a fly that moved it. You step and cast, and soon you're well past the point of action.

Looking upstream you realize that by following the current seam you've gradually waded out into the river, in a gentle left-curving arc that has kept you over the taking water. You've been fishing for about forty minutes, and you're down at the bottom of the run, where the river gets wider, flatter, and deeper. The water is still flowing at a good clip, but it's no longer rolling. This is a good place to change from the Green Machine to a size 6 single-hook Green Highlander, which will swing more lightly, especially in the slower water below.

You can't see down to the bottom, but here and there you can make out dark patches, probably large boulders. All the water in front of you looks good, and you'd like to cover as much as you can. The pool is wider here, but why not go for the home run? You're itching to unlimber your casting arm, you feel like you've got the rhythm of your casting stroke down pat, and there's plenty of room for your backcast. So you stay put and gradually lengthen your casts until you're throwing more than 50 feet of line.

You resume the cast-step-cast routine, casting beautifully. But in your desire to cover as much water as possible, you're instinctively reaching farther and farther across the river—that is, you're casting at an angle greater than 45 degrees. You're still getting a good swing when you make a good cast, but your efforts are getting sloppy. The fly almost always hits the water behind you on the backcast, because standing waist deep in the river brings you that much closer to the surface. And you're having a lot of trouble picking up the line from directly downstream and getting it to lay out straight on the forward cast, which you're making at an angle slightly wider than 45 degrees to the current.

A significant change of direction during a cast always robs the line of some of the energy it needs to straighten properly. Worse, when your fly lands with slack in the line it can't begin to swim effectively until the line comes taut. And oddly enough, the swing begins at a place you could cover easily with a 45-degree presentation on a shorter line. In other words, you're putting a mighty effort into reaching lies that you can't effectively cover.

An experienced caster can reorient the line with a false cast, but there's a much better and less tiring way to accomplish the same thing: a *water haul* (see fig. 7-4). With the fly on the dangle at the end of your cast, strip in a few handfuls of line. Without releasing the line in your hand, cast to a point midway between the point of pickup and your target area. Quickly snatch the cast back off the surface—the water haul—and shoot the line at the target.

Many fly fishers consider the water haul inelegant, but it's really an easy and effective way to improve both the angle and the length of your cast, enabling you to cover significantly more water. Although the water haul does disturb the surface, it happens over water you've already covered.

You quickly get the hang of this and continue to fish down. As you approach the heart of the pool, you wonder if you'll be able to cover the fish you saw roll earlier. You're now in slightly over your waist, struggling to keep your backcasts high and get a good swing across the main channel. This is where a two-handed rod would be a great asset, but you aren't fishing with one and your arm is getting tired.

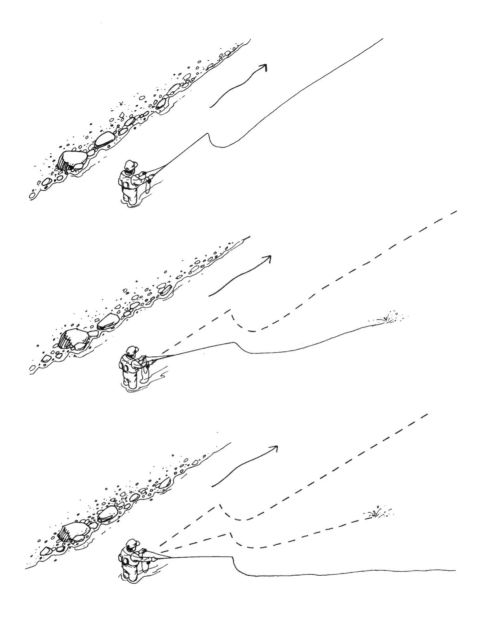

Figure 7-4. Water haul

As you strip off more line and cast, you notice that your lively connection to the river has gradually become dull and heavy. You have a lot of line out—over 60 feet—and even though the water is slower here, it puts a real bow in your rod. Another step, and the water is well over your waist. Obviously you won't be able to cover the left side of the main channel in the heart of the pool. You just hope that you cover the salmon that rolled before you run out of water to fish.

You keep edging forward, trying to find rocks on which to stand to gain a little more height. You squeeze three more casts out of the situation, but soon you're too tired to pop yet another good one. Your timing goes totally off and the fly and leader fall to the surface in a big nest.

Strip in your line and make sure the leader isn't wrapped around the fly in a way that ruins its action. Check your leader for *wind knots*— simple overhand knots that form in your leader from the wind or bad casting and greatly reduce its breaking strength. This is something you should do every time you make a lousy cast. In this situation, however, you won't make another cast. You're maxxed out, and you can use a rest.

As you wade directly back to shore, the water creeps toward the top of your waders. Finding this large eddy, or backwater, between you and the shore proves that you fished the water well, working your way down the gravel bar that separates the slow "turtle water" on the right from the main flow where salmon are likely to lie. But this slack water will also prevent you from continuing down through the pool when you're ready. You waded down the bar as far as you could go, effectively fishing all the taking water you could reach.

After a 20-minute break you walk down the bank, looking at the water. About 25 yards below the spot where you quit, the water near shore isn't quite as deep, and it seems to pick up a little speed. Beyond that you can make out the occasional dark shape of rocks under the surface. This is below the heart of the pool, and the bottom seems to have leveled off again. You can wade out and cover that water.

The Green Highlander is still a good choice, but a Muddler Minnow is a very good fly in gliding water and tailouts. You choose a size 6 double, because the twin hooks will stabilize the fly nicely in swifter water, and the fly's deer hair head will counteract the weight of the hook and give you plenty of buoyancy in the glide.

You patiently pick your way out as far as you can comfortably go, about 15 feet from shore. With any luck you'll be able to ease out farther as you work your way downstream in the broad bottom of the pool. It isn't necessary to fish a short line, because the water right in front of you is shallow and slow. Strip out enough line to reach beyond it, then resume your strip-and-cast regimen.

After three or four casts, you catch a limb behind you. Fortunately the 12-pound-test leader allows you to muscle out the fly with a few sharp snaps on the taut line. However, it's critical to examine both the fly and the leader after putting it through such stress. The Muddler seems fine; the hook points are still sharp. You visually check the leader for abrasions or nicks, then run it slowly between the pads of your thumb and index finger in case your eyes missed something.

The leader is fine, but you have a dilemma. If you're going to keep your backcast out of the trees, you have to fish at a 45-degree or smaller angle. But at that kind of angle, the river's leftward sweep means that even your best and longest cast barely gets you over the taking water (refer to fig. 7-1).

This isn't just a matter of wanting to cover as much water as possible; it's the critical issue of covering enough of the taking water to make your time and effort worthwhile. And the question of false casting is no longer just a matter of aesthetics. The trees on the bank won't allow you to get the distance you need.

The water haul is particularly handy here, because if you strip in all the line beyond the maximum backcast allowed by the trees, you never have to worry about hanging up. The length of line you can fish is easily determined by the maximum backcast the bank permits *plus* the amount of line you can shoot after your water haul. This demands cast-step-cast fishing, with your maximum length of line out.

Because you're fishing such a short line and using the water haul, you can easily fish at an angle approaching 90 degrees. And the larger the angle of your cast, the more potential fish you cover. However, the wide angle of your cast creates a new problem: *drag*. After your cast lands, the current sweeps the line downstream faster than the fly. When the line comes taut, the fly doesn't swing across slowly and steadily but instead races downstream and across, then comes to a dead stop below.

The only way to eliminate drag completely is to cast within the angle at which it begins to occur, an angle that will vary slightly with current speed: The faster the current, the sooner you'll experience drag when casting at an angle greater than 45 degrees. But you can also *mend* the

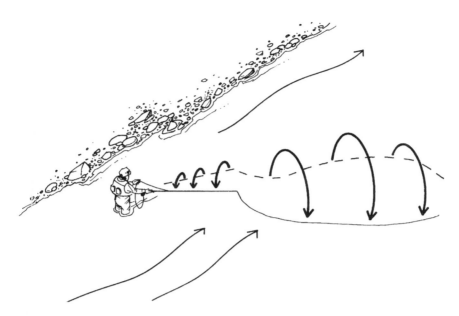

Figure 7-5. Mending line

line, a form of damage control that allows you to get a pretty good swing under unfavorable conditions—up to a point.

The mend is an easily executed mechanical attempt to give the fly a chance to get ahead of the line before it begins to drag (see fig. 7-5). As soon as the fly hits the water at the end of your cast, sharply make an upstream "hop" with your rod arm, lifting and moving a good part of your line upstream. Imagine standing at arm's length from a blackboard and quickly drawing the largest hemispherical curve that you can. This throws an upstream bag into the line, and by the time the line catches up, the fly is usually far enough downstream to swim across on a tight line at an acceptable pace.

Introducing all these articulations into your cast is work, but it pays off. You're covering more water than you thought you could, and you're doing so without having to worry about hanging up your backcast. After about 15 casts you've moved far enough downstream, and far enough out from the bank, not to have to worry about hanging up. Now you no longer step-and-cast but strip-and-cast, until you reach the maximum amount of line you can comfortably control in the air and on the water. Then you begin to water haul, adding length and angle. When the weight of the water on your line causes you to lose touch with the fly, you reel up a little, get back in touch, and fish that length with the step-cast-step method.

Once again you become immersed in the fishing. If your expectations are too high or your attention is too fierce, you will tire or become dejected much more quickly. This kind of fishing is about patience and stamina, and you need to pace yourself like a long-distance runner does, always watching for signs of possible interest in your fly.

The water approaching the tailout seems perfect. You can see most of the structure on the bottom now, and while wading over the rubble is tricky, the depth is fairly uniform clear across the river. The deepest part of the main channel is about three-quarters of the way over to the left bank, and it's just deep and swift enough to rule out any thought of crossing the river. By inching out into the river as you've waded down, you've gotten into a good position to cover the entire tailout, fishing at a comfortable 45-degree angle without using the water haul (refer to fig. 7-1).

The Muddler looks really enticing in the tailout, where the water slides like giant panes of glass over rough boulders of infinite shapes and sizes. Some are tall enough to cause disturbances on the surface, while in other places a good 4 feet of water flows over the aquatecture. From above, the tailout resembles a giant V pointing downstream, with all the water eventually channeled as standing waves over a break in the rugged stone formation that bisects the river and clearly marks the end of the pool.

After covering about half of the tailout, you notice that the current is so swift that your double-hook Muddler is sputtering and waking across the surface. This can be very enticing to salmon in slower water (see chapter 10), but when it occurs on a normal swing it usually indicates one of two things: Either your fly is too buoyant and water resistant, or the water is too swift to hold salmon, or both, for any length of time.

The tailout looks so fishy, and you've fished the pool so patiently, that you don't want to quit before you're done. So you switch to a more streamlined fly. You may have rolled a fish with the Green Machine and the Black and Blue in the run more than two hours earlier, but now the sun is high and bright and the water in the tailout is streamy and clear—ideal conditions for a small, sparse Silver Rat. You decide on a size 8 double.

This fly swims nicely in the swift tailout, but your hopes diminish with each step. You're hungry, and it's getting hot. Still, you fish slowly and carefully all the way down to the break. No luck. It's quitting time.

You wade back out to the shore, sit down on a large, flat boulder, eat a snack, then lie back and fall asleep in the shade. You wake up a little after 1 P.M. and contemplate your options. You could head downriver on foot, exploring a part of the Matapedia that flows well away from the road. You've always wanted to do that, but the next named pool is easily accessible from the road only about ¾ mile downstream, and you decide against it. You'd just be slogging through a long series of riffles and white-water breaks that offer no holding lies, and where you'd have no chance of spotting fish.

It seems wiser to head back to the cabin, stopping at a few strategic pullouts or high banks along the way. If you spot a fish, you can work it with a dry fly. If not, you can get out of your waders, have a shower and a bite of lunch, and plan the rest of your day's fishing, trying to maximize your chances for the evening.

But first, on the way back to the car, you're going to take another shot at the "maybe" fish up in the run. It's tempting to try the Green

A large salmon fresh from the sea prior to release. Catch-and-release is a proven conservation strategy that is mandated on salmon rivers from eastern Canada and New England to Russia's Kola Peninsula (Photo: Val Atkinson)

Machine again, or maybe that good choice that the fish hasn't seen yet, the Silver Rat. But you're partial to the Black and Blue. Maybe the salmon will come back to it.

The rock with the quartz marking isn't obvious from the path and you have to poke around a little on the shore until you find it. You want to get the best swing possible on the ideal length of line, so you wade out into the river about 6 feet below the rock so that you can cover the fish with a sweet, easily managed cast. Estimating the length of cast required to cover the fish would be risky, so you start with a short line and lengthen until you cover the fish.

As you cast, you realize how hard it is to pinpoint the precise area where the fish took—not to mention where it was before it rolled for your fly or whether or not it was even a salmon. Never mind all that, because suddenly there's a huge boil in the water below the tip of your fly line, your arm is pulled toward the water, and line flows from your reel to the slow click, click, click of the drag.

Congratulations. You've hooked a salmon.

APPLIED KNOWLEDGE

Let's take a closer look at some of the key elements in our idealized scenario. You did a very good job of angling, but one big tactical decision of yours could be challenged. Usually it makes sense to fish a pool from the top down, especially on public water, where you could lose your chance to be the first through a pool if other anglers arrive. But there are a few factors and options worth contemplating before you start to fish.

Once the water levels begin to subside and water temperatures begin to rise during the warm, bright days of summer, you'll most likely find salmon in tailout areas early in the day, in deeper parts of the main channel as the day goes on, and up in the run at the head of the pool in the evening. It would be an error to take this as an ironclad rule, but do keep it in mind.

For instance, if the pool you want to fish early in the morning is very long and there are two anglers up at the head, you have an opportunity to fish the tail at the time when it's most likely to produce. Just make sure you don't crowd the other anglers (see chapter 11). Conversely, even though the tailout of Matalik looked terrific, you were fishing it at the time of day when it's less likely to produce.

I've seen or caught salmon in all three main areas of a pool—head, heart, tail—at every time of day, and to some degree an ideal lie is good all the time. However, salmon generally don't like bright sunlight and thin, warm water, and in such conditions they tend to move into the deepest, coolest, most oxygenated water available. In many cases salmon will rest in tailouts briefly after entering a pool, then slowly make their way up the pool into more comfortable lies.

By the same token, as evening approaches fish work their way up into or within runs, ready to move upstream at dusk. In pools that begin with a tumultuous riffle (instead of a long, steady run), the most over-looked area is the very top of the pool, just below the riffle. Fish stage there late in the day before moving on, and they often rest there at other hours as well because of the oxygen supplied by the riffle.

In the best of all worlds and under the conditions described above, you'd fish Matalik *backward*—that is, fish the top and bottom the same way, but in reverse order. This conflicts with the basic logic of down-stream wet-fly fishing, but remember that in this case you actually fished two distinct areas as if they were different pools.

What length of cast you should fish is always an important issue. Most of the time you need at least 10 feet of line and leader to give you a good swing. Once you get beyond 50 feet you start losing touch with the fly, or pool and current conditions may make it hard to get that tight, slow swing so critical to success.

I've watched dozens of experienced anglers in canoes struggling to make their longest casts, although they could've covered fish more effec-tively and easily by dropping the boat down more often. Wading anglers also strive for that long line and commit another strategic error in the process: making very long casts at 45-degree angles when a much shorter line, with a little more upstream angle, would cover the same amount of water. Casting a long line doesn't necessarily cover more good water, it's a lot more tiring, and you lose tight control of your line and fly.

The two factors used in determining the length of line you should fish are, in order, the quality of your swing and the amount of taking water you can cover. If you must compromise, give up water rather than swing quality. You're better off fishing one-third of a pool very well than three-quarters of it indifferently. With a little experience you'll be able to identify the taking water in most pools, and you should try to fish it with your most effective cast and swing.

In many pools, and particularly in runs, this means that you should begin the cast-step-cast march downstream long before you hit your maximum reliable cast. If the water and the quality of your swing suggest that you begin to cast-step-cast with just 25 feet of line out, do it.

If you have trouble persuading your casting arm that length for length's sake is a mistake, consider this: Far more fish are lost when they're hooked on a long line, because the spongy resistance of all that line prevents the rod and angler from properly setting the hook. It's a shame to lose a fish that was poorly hooked with 75 feet of line out when you would've eventually covered and solidly hooked the same fish with 50 feet.

Always remember that opening up your angle and making a quick mend after every cast will in many cases allow you to cover much more water, and more effectively, than adding length. Making a useful mend in a relatively short line is easy, while attempting to mend a long line often accomplishes nothing, because the energy of the mending action expires long before it reaches the tip of the line.

One technique you can try in some situations is the *reach cast*—essentially a mend made in midair, before your line hits the water. End your forward cast with maximum arm extension, then move your arm and rod as far upstream as you can, with a motion similar to that used for mending line on the water, before the cast lands (see fig. 7-6). With the reach cast, the line lands on the water at a much more pronounced downstream angle.

The mend and reach casts aren't merely damage-control devices intended to offset drag but techniques that add to the fly's effective swing time. While the reach cast can be very effective in swift water, the traditional mend works best in slower water.

It isn't easy to tell when a bump, twitch, or rap on your line is a rise from a salmon. Generally, parr take exactly the way their larger brethren do, but on a different scale: You'll feel only a light rap and the immediate wriggling of the hooked little fish. The same is true of resident trout,

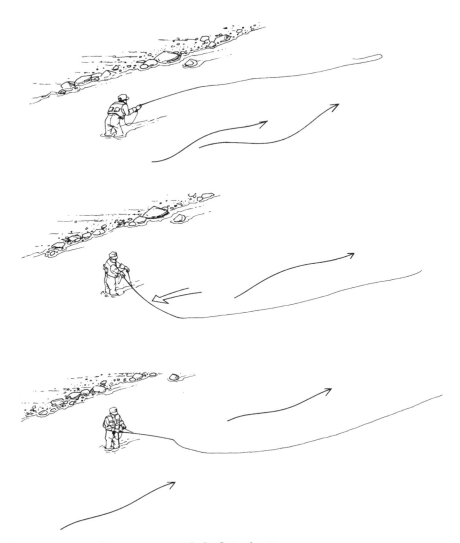

Figure 7-6. Reach cast, starting with the fly in the air

although sea-run trout, especially ones that weigh over 2 pounds, take much like salmon do.

One thing to keep in mind, however, is that salmon are usually large enough to make some kind of surface disturbance when they take or even roll to a fly. In low water this may be a dramatic boil, a spectacular splash, or the sight of the fish's head or back poking through the surface. In medium to high water salmon often take without any sign on the surface. In fact under such conditions a surface disturbance sometimes indicates that the fly is moving too quickly for a fish that isn't feeling particularly aggressive. (For more on this, see chapter 9.)

Shortening up on a rolled fish is one of the most effective and unacknowledged techniques for hooking short-takers, even though it runs contrary to an angler's instincts or even logic. I've hooked many fish that I rolled by shortening up and rarely hooked fish by lengthening line. Just why is open to speculation, but I'm convinced that aggressive salmon are more comfortable moving slightly upstream to take a fly.

Theories aside, it's clear that fishing a shorter line as your first strategy has no downside. If the fish you rolled was a late-taker, or if in some way your previous cast wasn't enticing, fishing a shorter line gives the salmon a better look the second time around. Besides, if shortening up doesn't work you'll still cover the same fish with the cast that originally triggered a response, and even with longer ones. But remember: Shortening up is a matter of inches.

Most anglers fishing a wet fly simply follow it through a swing with the rod pointed at it and the tiptop near the surface of the water. But on some rivers anglers like to *pump* the fly, rhythmically raising and lowering the rod about a foot as the fly swings around. This pumping action gives the fly a darting motion that advocates swear by, although there's no hard evidence to suggest that fish consistently find a pumped fly more appealing.

I usually pump a wet fly unless the water is swift and rolling, and even then I'll pump if I'm getting a great, slow swing. In flat, slower water, pumping seems to keep the fly moving at a crisp pace on a tight line. The pumping motion also seems to enhance the appeal of some wet flies, most notably the Butterfly. I like the simple cadence of pumping the fly, too. Incidentally, there comes a point when you can actually feel that pumping no longer has an effect on the fly. This is a pretty good indication that you have too much line out.

Thus successful wet-fly fishing is not simply a matter of mastering the basic down-and-across, step-cast-step technique, but also one of constantly seeking to maximize the fly's productive drift, along with basic rivercraft and eternal vigilance.

CHAPTER 8

Fishing the Dry Fly

Compared to classic wet-fly fishing, the use of dry flies requires a very different sensibility, in both general and specific ways. Generally, dry flies are fished dead drift, across or quartering upstream, with the fly taking the same path through the current as might a free-floating wood chip. Although combing the water with a dry fly occasionally produces fish, you can't cover a pool as precisely, thoroughly, or quickly as you can by fishing a wet fly downstream and across. The wet fly is a marvelously effective prospecting tool. The dry fly is at its lethal best when fished to a specific target—a lie or a fish.

In medium and low water, the rule of thumb with wet flies is: The smaller the better. But under the same conditions, the dry fly of choice is a large (long-shank size 4 or 6) Bomber. With a dry fly, outlandish size, appearance, and even color may goad a reluctant salmon into taking. With a wet fly, this works so rarely that it's seldom even attempted.

There are various popular notions about the "right" time to fish a dry fly, the most common being not to bother unless the air is warmer than the water. Don't believe it. While it's true that salmon won't move very far through fast, cold, deep water to take a dry fly, I'll still try a floating fly even in the early season if I can get a relatively slow float over a fish, particularly one holding in a shallow lie. The dry fly is potentially deadly almost anytime, particularly on visible fish.

To me salmon seem almost passionate about dry flies, often reacting to them much more strongly than to wet flies. Of course genuine passion is never easily aroused, and you can't expect to fish just any old dry fly any old way and get results. But the right dry fly fished the right way often moves fish that are indifferent to wet flies.

Dry flies may provoke more curiosity from salmon as well as make them feel more threatened; a dry fly can more effectively and repetitively invade their "space." And because dry flies are less dependent on swing, or current speed and consistency than wet flies, you can make precise, attractive presentations to more fish under a greater variety of water conditions. You can't cover as *much* water with a dry fly, but you can thoroughly cover specific places and fish from a far greater variety of angles, employing an astonishing number of techniques. The following anecdote touches on some of these points.

In the summer of 1995 I was fishing the legendary Pavilion water on the Gaspe's Ste. Jean River with Richard Franklin and Atlantic Salmon Federation president Bill Taylor. The Pavilion may be the greatest dry-fly water in all of Canada, because of the quality of its holding pools and the remarkable purity and clarity of its water. (And it's open to the public, albeit on a limited basis decided by lottery—a strategy that keeps this wonderful wilderness stretch of river from being overrun and degraded.)

On our final morning, Richard and I were assigned to fish together in Big Indian Pool. This is the last holding pool downstream from a cross-stream barrier designed to keep fish from moving upstream (and into the range of poachers) until spawning time. Every fish ascending the Ste. Jean ultimately reaches the fence and then must drop back. From early July on, Big Indian commonly holds more than 100 salmon, most of them easily visible.

Under recent Quebec regulations you're done fishing for the day after you've killed or released one salmon. As my guide, Wayne Miller, and I approached Big Indian, I was thinking mainly of ways to enjoy a

The River Ste. Jean (Photo: Richard Franklin)

little extra fishing time in this extraordinary environment before I caught and released my salmon and had to quit. The Pavilion water is one of the few places in all salmon fishing where this degree of arrogance is justified.

Big Indian begins with a swift riffle that becomes a glide, then gradually curves into a very deep, still pool flanked by old bridge abutments. As I stood on the gravel beach at the head of Big Indian, I was struck by the strange, dark formations of ledgerock visible in the river. Then I realized that these "ledges" were actually the backs of salmon.

I wandered down along the beach to the glide. There were fish everywhere. Earlier in the trip a New Brunswick judge, John Turnbull, had given me a Burdock dry fly—a coarse brown cousin of the Bomber—and I tied it on. Savoring each moment, I fished to the largest salmon, one by one, gradually moving upstream toward the fast water. Two days earlier Bill and I had each landed and released salmon with the Burdock; in fact Bill's fish had been the third to rise to his fly in a single drift. But now, two days later, I couldn't get a fish even to twitch a fin.

No problem. I snipped off the Burdock and tied on one of my own favorites, a size 6 green Buck Bug with brown hackle and a stubby tail of green sparkle yarn. The fish were visible, the casting was easy, but the salmon might indeed have been ledges for all the interest they showed. Next I tried a standard Bomber. Nothing. Was it possible to do everything in my power and still get skunked on a pool so thick with fish? Although I prefer dry flies, an experiment was in order. I fished a size 10 Green Machine wet fly all the way down from the very head of the riffle. Again, neither Wayne nor I saw any reactions from the fish.

Soon it was nearly noon. The sun burned high overhead—the Gaspe was in the grasp of a brutal heat wave—and afternoon fishing seemed neither attractive nor promising. Meanwhile, using his considerable trout fishing savvy, Richard had scored on a long downstream presentation over a large pod of salmon suspended in the still, deep heart of the pool. A 10-pounder broke ranks, swam up, and took the green Bomber. Richard released it and was done for the day. I was getting skunked on as near to a "can't-miss" situation as you'll find in fishing.

I finally tied on the closest thing I have to a secret weapon—a large orange Bomber with brown hackle and a tuft of white calf tail protruding fore and aft. I started at the bottom of the glide, fishing

Releasing a salmon back into the River Ste. Jean (Photo: Richard Franklin)

upstream. On my fourth or fifth cast, a salmon rushed the fly just as I was picking it off the water. Three casts later, a different salmon tried to take it, but missed.

Four more casts, and a fish bolted 10 feet from a lie near the far bank, the white insides of its gaping mouth clearly visible as it engulfed the fly. I landed this strong 12-pounder, amazed once again at the unpredictability of salmon fishing.

This anecdote illustrates the importance of hitting on a hot color or style of dry fly. Of course the orange Bomber's dramatic appeal may have had less to do with the fly's color or nature than with the specific conditions of the moment. It's entirely possible that an hour earlier or later, under different conditions of light and visibility, the orange Bomber would've been ignored.

Although I've had many similar experiences, I can abstract only one general theory from them: Dry-fly salmon fishing is a trial-and-error undertaking that operates most successfully within the parameters of a specific river. In other words, every river has proven patterns and colors for specific conditions. Those flies have earned the right to get not just a fair chance but often the first chance. Still, you should always be willing to experiment, especially with large and colorful flies.

Now that we've established that dry-fly fishing for salmon can be a wildly random enterprise, I have to take you one step further—even though after it you may decide that fishing dry flies for salmon is a riddle wrapped in an enigma, tucked into a conundrum, stamped with uncertainty, and lost in the mail.

I've caught plenty of salmon that rushed out of nowhere to hammer a fly, and I've had a few other experiences like the one on the Ste. Jean. But most of the fish I've caught on the surface took my dry fly after numerous presentations, often as if something about one specific cast finally proved too much for them to resist. So despite my aversion to most theories of salmon behavior, I've come to embrace one as gospel truth.

THE SACRED INCH

Consistent success with the dry fly hinges upon a very specific concept of presentation, first articulated by George LaBranche in his seminal work,

The Salmon and the Dry Fly (Scribner's, New York, 1924). LaBranche was an angling companion of Colonel Ambrose Monell, who leased a long stretch of the same river where I learned to fish salmon, the Upsalquitch. This river is perfect dry-fly water, and it's no wonder that LaBranche and Monell became the pioneers of dry-fly fishing for salmon.

LaBranche believed that the surface of every pool is a complex area full of minute currents, which he called *grooves*. To LaBranche, raising a salmon to a dry fly meant placing the fly on what he called the *sacred inch*—the one groove upon which the fly became irresistible to a taking fish.

LaBranche was a formidable and knowledgeable trout fisherman, and his sacred-inch theory reveals a trout fisher's empirical sensibility. But this is salmon fishing. I don't want to play fast and loose with LaBranche's theory, but in my experience it's usually impossible to divine the precise location of the sacred inch by just looking at the water. It isn't necessarily the spot where the current takes your drifting fly over the fish; it may not even always be in the same place. And a fly drifting into the sacred inch may not be as appealing as one that alights on it; one that alights on it may not be as effective as one that skitters across stream onto it.

To understand the novelty and importance of LaBranche's theory, imagine that a salmon you're fishing to is looking through a kaleidoscope; each cast represents a twist of the barrel. Usually the fly is broken up and blends into the background, indistinguishable from other particles of light and color. But when a fly alights on the sacred inch, it suddenly comes into sharp focus and becomes a fabulously irresistible object.

I don't believe that placing a fly on the sacred inch will get all or even most salmon to take. But I'm convinced that placing a fly anywhere else decreases your chances in direct proportion to its distance from the sacred inch.

I mentioned earlier that the dry fly is most effective when fished to a target, and the best target of all is a visible fish. For this reason I spend a lot of time just looking for salmon. When the fishing is slow or if I've fished hard all morning, I'll often spend parts of the slow midday period between 11 and 4 looking for fish, even if I've shed my waders and broken down my rod.

After fishing a wet fly through a productive pool, I almost always fish back up with a dry fly, water conditions permitting. This makes angling sense, particularly if you plan to fish through the pool again with a different wet fly. Why waste time walking back up to the head of the pool when you could fish your way up as quickly—or slowly—as you wish, while keeping a fly on the water? This also breaks up the tedium that can accompany wet-fly fishing on a slow day. The mere sight of a jaunty dry fly—and the anticipation it generates—gives you a refreshing boost. And if you fish the dry fly properly, you'll cover a lot of the taking water much more quickly than you did on the way down.

MATALIK: PROSPECTING THE WATER

Let's return briefly to the Matapedia's Matalik Pool, which you fished with the wet fly in chapter 7. And let's assume that you fished it thoroughly with the wet fly from top to bottom without rolling a fish.

Matalik's tailout, with its profusion of structure, is good dry-fly water. The choice of fly is a no-brainer: the Bomber. All things being equal, a medium to large Bomber should always be your first choice. And remember: With a dry fly you must be ready to strike at the moment a fish takes the fly (more on this in chapter 9).

Take stock of the tailout, carefully looking for fish and identifying specific lies that might hold them around boulders, groups of rocks, or variations in the riverbed indicated by a change in water color: Darker water is always deeper water. Salmon rarely lie smack in the center of depressions or other eccentric riverbed features; they usually take up positions on the perimeter.

Fish the closest targets first, making at least four casts to a specific lie (see fig. 8-1). The first cast should cover the near downstream side of the lie, the second the near upstream side, the third the far downstream side, and the fourth the far upstream side. This way you're placing a decent first cast in each attractive zone rather than showing the fly to fish outside your target area. This is important, because when you're prospecting for fish you can't see, your first cast represents your best chance.

In dark water with no single piece of visible structure, drift the fly through the gut of the area, with your first cast at the near edge of the

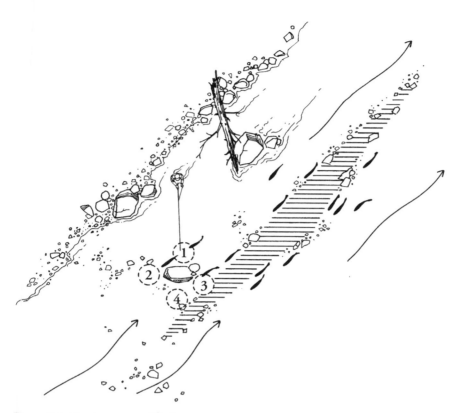

Figure 8-1. Casting to a specific lie

trough and the last cast over the far edge. Keep false casting to a minimum, and resist the urge to drift your fly down into the taking area from too far upstream. Try to drop the fly just a few inches above the area you want to cover.

After you've covered all the potential lies within your casting range, begin moving upstream, continuing to hit specific targets. As you move up out of the tailout, the water you're covering gets deeper and the structure becomes less visible. Move along more quickly. Get a few nice long drifts right through the heart of the pool and along any reachable current seam. You'll find yourself covering water that you couldn't fish effectively with the wet fly. But unless you have a lot of time, don't comb the slow, dark water. Go up to the run.

Dry-fly fishing in swift water calls for a change of technique. In general salmon are much more inclined to rise to a fly that lands just a few inches in front of them than one that comes drifting down from far upstream. In fact the longer your fly drifts, the less likely you are to raise a fish. The exception to this rule is when drag serendipitously sets in at the moment a fly is over a salmon well downstream of you. The fly's sudden movement sometimes triggers a take.

In rolling water, particularly where there is no conspicuous target area, you're much better off fishing short cross-stream casts than casting far upstream and striving for the long, drag-free drifts typical of trout fishing. Remember, unlike trout, salmon aren't spooked by your proximity or by drag; sometimes drag on a dry fly even induces them to take, as long as it's the kind of drag that makes a fly skitter and appear alive and *not* the moderate drag that occurs when an angler is trying too hard to get a natural float on a long line in swift water.

So forget elegant upstream casts and long drifts. Even if you raise a fish, all that slack line will make it nearly impossible for you to set the hook well. Fish short and fish fast. Drop casts here and there, dapping the fly into every identifiable current seam. Fish the dry fly as if you were making an impressionist painting, with apparently random dollops of color that add up to a recognizable image.

In the rolling water, make two or three casts over any variation in river color you find; such patches almost always indicate structure, and sometimes the gray ones are actually fish. And watch closely for a flash of silver or the splash of a salmon moving for your fly. When a fish moves in swift water, it will often come back if you cover it well.

HOME POOL: FISHING TO VISIBLE SALMON

Prospecting with a dry fly is a pleasant change from the meticulous, meditative process of combing the water with a wet fly. But there's nothing quite like fishing the dry fly to visible salmon. And this brings us back to another pool we've visited before, Home Pool on the Upsalquitch. The Upsalquitch still provides something very much like lab conditions for dry-fly anglers, as it did during the salad years of Monell and LaBranche. Because of this I think of the Upsalquitch as the ultimate in dry-fly fishing, and the lessons I've learned there have served me well on other rivers, even under very different conditions.

On a typical morning on Home Pool, Shane Mann and I get in the canoe in the pool's tailout (refer to fig. 6-1) and motor slowly up along the right bank. Dry-fly fishing for salmon is a two-stage process: locating a fish, then inducing it to take. Toward this end Shane stands on his seat in the stern, and I usually stand on the other seat, both of us peering into the water for salmon. Shane always spots them first, and I listen to his litany as we motor through the pool.

"There's a grilse over by that yellow rock. Whoa, there's *three* grilse. Uh, uh, uh—there's a salmon lying right against the ledges. Oh, oh, oh, oh—there's a mighty fish just this side of that light piece of bottom, behind that black rock right in the middle."

After we see what's in the pool we drift slowly back down, staying as close to the right bank as possible. Shane drops the anchor well above the place where we spotted our first fish. Standing on the seat and paying out line, he inches the canoe downstream until the fish comes into view. Then he snubs the bow line, parking us slightly upstream and across from the fish.

I try not to cast until I see the salmon myself, which sometimes takes a fair amount of direction from Shane. Once I locate it I take stock of conditions, because I want to make my best presentation with my first cast. A good first cast doesn't guarantee a take, but it often provokes a response that lets you know whether a fish is active and catchable. Conversely, a bad first cast that lands way beyond the fish or smacks the water above its dorsal fin seems to rob you of the vital element of surprise, establishing the fly as something already seen and thus neither novel, threatening, or worthy of the salmon's attention.

We usually try a standard Bomber first, placing it about 12 to 18 inches upstream and just to the near side of the salmon's head. I believe this is the most common location for the sacred inch, although LaBranche and his companions preferred to drop the fly farther upstream, allowing it to drift into the critical area. I feel that the invasive nature of a closer cast often triggers a reflexive take, one so swift that you can feel in your bones the automatic nature of the salmon's response.

If this invasive cast, perfectly executed, fails to raise the fish, I try it again and again. Shane comments on each cast as it falls, giving me a good idea of my accuracy. Even under the best of conditions (short cast, still air), three casts out of four alight just far enough off target to be discounted. Thus it takes about 20 casts to make a half-dozen decent presentations. Keep in mind that finding the sacred inch is all about precision, even when it occurs through good luck rather than skill.

Given the sheer number of errant casts, it's tempting to pick up the bad ones as soon as they hit the water. Ripping the fly off the water near a fish won't spook it; occasionally this even stirs it up and makes it more disposed to take. But usually undue commotion merely conditions a fish to disturbance and makes it less and less vulnerable to the novelty of the fly. Let every cast drift until it is well below the fish, then try to lift the fly off the water gently.

Current-induced surface irregularities can neutralize the effect of the best sacred-inch cast or enhance the appeal of a comparatively poor one. Flat, deep, relatively slow-moving water is often free of surface irregularities. But briskly moving water above varied structure is full of inconsistencies: momentary upwellings, passing whirlpools, and sometimes entire "panels" of flat water that slide by, giving you a clear, moving window to the bottom.

These surface characteristics create the kaleidoscopic background I mentioned earlier, and they profoundly affect the way a salmon sees a fly. Depending on what's happening on the surface, the sacred inch may come and go or exist briefly in different areas near a fish. This may explain in part why so many salmon take a dry fly after ignoring numerous, seemingly identical presentations. I believe that a dry fly dropped into one of those smooth panels is especially enticing.

If a fish doesn't react to my invasive casts, I begin to probe around for the sacred inch. After resting the fish for a minute, I cast about 3 feet upstream of it and give it a different, longer look at the fly, letting the current take the fly where it will. Accuracy is not as critical with this probing cast, because you want the current to present the fly to the salmon at a variety of angles. I vary each cast slightly and lengthen just a bit so that I can get a good drift on the far side of the fish. Sometimes a strong sun, even early in the day, will discourage a fish from rising to a fly presented on its bright side.

All the while Shane keeps up his running commentary. A good guide is always watching the water, judging every cast you make and observing every reaction of the fish. Salmon show a remarkable range of responses to a fly, from absolute indifference (even to a large fly splatted down right over their heads) to hell-bent fury that sends them rocketing through 5 feet of water after a small fly serenely drifting along. Between those extremes lies an infinite range of reactions, all of them offering hope.

Salmon that show no reaction from the get-go, particularly when you've started off with a few good casts, are often impossible. But fish that show some interest, even if it's only a lazy levitation of 2 or 3 inches toward the surface, are often taking fish. In general, the more agitated the salmon, the more likely they are to take the fly—or another one—sooner or later.

Of course there are those fish that chase a fly, slash or swirl at it, or even roll over it without ever taking it. I once fished over a grilse in slow water for the better part of an hour, getting only the mildest of encouraging signs. Sometimes it would move to one side or the other as the fly drifted over. Other times it seemed to tip its nose up, as if it wanted a slightly better look. Finally the fish rose with agonizing leisure to the green and yellow Bomber, took it by the hackles, tugged it under water, then released it—all without ever touching the hook. Working a coy fish can be frustrating, but usually it's an absorbing, challenging enterprise worth pursuing as long as you find it interesting.

Salmon usually react to a dry fly at one of three levels. The first we'll call *curiosity*, usually manifested as measured interest. Curious fish may move off their lies to get a better look at a fly, or they may slowly rise up and inspect it. They might even drift along for a few inches or feet just below it.

The second level is *agitation*. This is a higher, more active level of interest. Agitated fish may bolt at a fly or, after allowing it to drift over them, turn and chase it without actually grabbing it. These excited—and exciting—reactions often create a surface disturbance near the fly.

The third level is *commitment*. This is the reaction of a taking fish, and there's very little you can do to keep a dry fly away from a salmon that really wants it.

Although these three levels of interest seem progressive, it's surprising how often they aren't. It's difficult to push a curious fish into a state of agitation, and it's only slightly less difficult to turn an agitated fish into a committed fish, despite the natural connection between those states.

It's also just as unlikely that an agitated fish will suddenly become merely curious. There's a far better chance that it will become utterly indifferent. Often fish seem locked into the first two states: Each similar reaction to a fly cast to the same spot increases the odds of a similar or lesser reaction to a similar cast with the same fly.

If and when a salmon makes a pass at a fly, it's critical to allow sufficient time for the fish to resettle in its lie before making another cast—which isn't always easy in the electric moment after a fish moves for your fly. Even a salmon that rushed furiously at your fly usually takes its own sweet time returning to its lie. If you can't see the fish, give it a slow count of at least 10 before casting again.

When a fish responds to a fly sporadically, it may mean it isn't getting the same look at the fly each time, even if each cast appears to fall in the same place. This may or may not be in your control. When a salmon reacts to a fly a few times in succession, however, it usually means you've found the sacred inch, but for one reason or another the fish is reluctant. You don't want to lock the salmon into its own disinclination. This is a good time to change flies and to rest the fish.

Shane and I usually try a fly substantially different in size and color from the original at this point, and return to square one—an invasive presentation. If the fish reacts to the new fly exactly as it did to the old, getting that fish will likely prove very tough. This is especially true if the reaction is tepid. No reaction is often preferable to the same reaction, because this may indicate that the fish finds one fly more attractive than the other.

Although Shane and I have tried as many as a dozen different dry flies over the same fish, the most reliable way to move seemingly indifferent fish is not a change of fly but a change of presentation. Curious or agitated salmon can be pushed over the brink by any of a number of radical

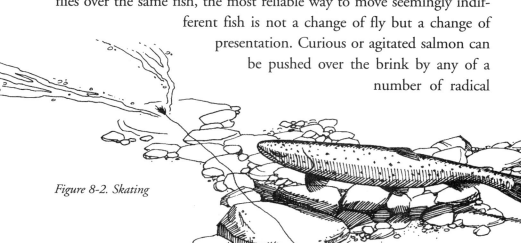

Figure 8-2. Skating

presentations. Salmon that ignore a drifting fly, or show only passing interest in it, will often wallop one dramatically presented.

My most effective alternate technique is *skating* (see fig. 8-2). Cast the fly about 10 feet beyond the fish, then smoothly drag it back over the surface, holding the line in one hand and lifting the rod with the other. Stop the fly right above the salmon's nose.

Skittering is a variation on skating; you just impart more action by jiggling the rod as you skate the fly across the surface. You can also drop a cast about 3 feet upstream, or the same distance upstream and beyond the fish, and give the fly a brisk jiggle or tug a moment after it lands, twitching or dragging it into the window just above and forward of the fish.

Another unorthodox presentation that has worked well for me is the *splat cast,* which works best with smaller flies such as Buck Bugs. The trick is to smack the Bug down on the water, as hard as you can, right on top of the salmon's head. When this cast is well executed you'll actually hear the Bug "plop."

One of the most common alternate ploys involves teasing a salmon by dropping the fly just inches upstream and immediately snatching it off the water as many as a dozen times in rapid succession—almost as if you're trying to simulate an insect hatch (albeit a strange one). Finally, try dropping the fly about 6 feet upstream and allowing a long, natural float down over the fish. This one has never worked for me, but I still try it from time to time.

Fishing six flies (a reasonable number) through an effective range of presentations over one fish can consume an hour, but that time flies by when the salmon is a bright and interested 20-pounder. On Home Pool, a number of fish are usually present; this not only ensures that we're always working on fish but also demands that we fish comprehensively and efficiently.

Sometimes an active salmon simply won't commit to taking the fly. It's easy to become obsessed with such a fish; always remember, however, that the more predictable and patterned your strategy becomes, the more your chances diminish.

It's very important to rest a fish, especially if you've been working it steadily. Most fish can be rested for as long as it takes to tie on a new fly.

But with an agitated fish that has come to your fly a few times, it's often more productive to rest it longer—at least 10 or 15 minutes, although a half hour is better, and ninety minutes is ideal. In these situations, I've had my best luck reusing the first fly to get a response. In fact, I rarely quit on a fish that has shown interest without making one last try with my original fly. This tactic has been surprisingly successful.

The most important thing I've learned on Home Pool is that, even on a great, private stretch of water, salmon on the dry fly are rarely easy. Most of the fish we raise aren't committed to taking a fly; on the rare occasions when they are, the fishing isn't very challenging. This lesson has really boosted my confidence on public water, because it means that even if a pool has been fished hard, it may not have been fished right, or with sufficient persistence and deliberation.

Granted, a wading angler, or one on water where it's hard to spot fish, will find it more difficult to practice ultimate dry-fly fishing than one fishing from a canoe, with a guide, on a clear river. But no matter where you are, if you work specific, visible fish with a variety of flies and techniques, your chances of catching salmon with dries will skyrocket.

POPULAR ATLANTIC SALMON FLIES

Copper Killer *(tied by George Kesel)*

Canadian Black Dose *(tied by George Kesel)*

Silver Doctor *(tied by Harry Perkins)*

Nighthawk *(tied by Mark Favorite)*

Green Highlander *(tied by Teddy Waterman)*

Heron Spey Fly *(tied by Mark Favorite)*

Rusty Rat *(tied by Danny Bird)*

Silver Rat *(tied by Danny Bird)*

Cosseboom *(tied by Danny Bird)*

Black Bear Greenbutt *(tied by Dan Fitzgerald)*

Undertaker *(tied by Warren Duncan)*

Black & Blue *(tied by Jim Emery)*

Lady Joan *(tied by Danny Bird)*

Orange Blossom *(tied by Danny Bird)*

Monroe Killer *(tied by Danny Bird)*

Green Machine
(tied by Danny Bird)

Butterfly *(tied by Warren Duncan)*

RECOMMENDED FOR RUSSIAN WATERS

General Practitioner *(tied by Warren Duncan)*

Allie's Shrimp *(tied by George Cote)*

DRY FLIES

Royal Wulff *(tied by Carl Yoshida)*

White Wulff *(tied by Danny Bird)*

Brown Bomber *(tied by Carl Yoshida)*

THE FOLLOWING FLIES HAVE BEEN TIED WITH KRYSTAL FLASH RATHER THAN IN THE TRADITIONAL STYLE OF USING REAL MATERIALS. THEY WORK JUST AS WELL.

Louise *(tied by Jim Emery)*

Glitter Bear—Bird version *(tied by Danny Bird)*

Green Glitter Bug *(tied by Danny Bird)*

Salmon Muddler *(tied by Ellis Hatch)*

All color photography by Richard Franklin.
Special thanks to Nick Wilder at Hunter's Angling Supplies for all his help in selection.

CHAPTER 9

Hooking and Playing, Landing and Releasing

If you've never caught a large gamefish on a fly, all the advice in the world can't prepare you for the feeling of hooking your first salmon. Even if you've caught fish of similar size and strength—striped bass, bluefish, pike—the Atlantic salmon has a weapon they often don't: its environment. A swift river is full of forces and features a fish can use against you. The good news is that such elements can also be made to work for you.

To subdue salmon skillfully and humanely, there are three cardinal rules to follow:

- Don't panic.
- Don't be timid.
- Don't ever be afraid to lose the fish.

It's amazing how often beginning and even experienced anglers become paralyzed at the sight and feel of a large salmon taking a fly. Suddenly there's a great swirl and a surge of live weight travels immediately through your rod arm to your brain, which translates it into *Ohmygod, I've got hold of something I'm not sure I can handle.*

It's incredible how well a 9-foot rod conveys a fish's strength, explosive power, and untamed nature. It's as though the rod levels the playing field, providing you an intimate connection with an essentially unknowable wild creature. If you panic, you'll be denied the fullness of that experience—a fancy way of saying that you'll lose the fish and the rewards that go with it.

Once you get yourself under control, you need to get the fish under control. You can only do this by overcoming your fear of pressuring your tackle and the fish. The typical salmon outfit will bear a lot more stress than you think. Many more anglers lose fish by being timid than by applying too much pressure. In fact even with a 12-pound-test leader and a 9-by-9 rod, applying too much pressure is virtually impossible, unless you're *trying* to break something. I can't give you the hands-on experience you need, but later I'll describe some techniques that will allow you to get the most out of your gear.

Remember that there are two kinds of salmon anglers: Those who've lost fish, and those who're going to lose fish. Lost fish, especially *big* fish, are both part of the angling experience and one of the risks that make fly fishing a fair-chase sport and not a simple act of harvest. You'll always second-guess yourself after losing a fish, and you'll invariably lose some fish because of angler error or gear failure. But most fish are lost simply due to bad luck—a chance you accepted when you elected to fish with a fly instead of a hand grenade.

Fishing buddies and bank-dwelling experts may say you lost a fish because you were using a single hook instead of a double, or because you exerted too much or too little pressure, or because you struck too early, too late, or not at all. And sometimes they'll be right. But often you lose fish for reasons beyond your control. Accept it as part of the game.

At some moment in the struggle with a salmon, especially a great salmon, you may need to pressure the fish more than seems comfortable. As we'll see later in this chapter, your decisions should be based less on the fear of losing the fish by applying too much pressure than on the fear of losing it by applying too little. In other words, if a fish is headed for a spot where it will be impossible to land, it's worth the risk to apply whatever pressure is needed to stop it. Let's look at a real-life situation to illustrate these issues.

Joe and Edgar Cullman, have a spectacular camp on the Upsalquitch called Two Brooks, about 12 river miles above Maclennan Lodge. The only access to this camp is via a badly rutted dirt road, then a short boat ride across the river to a near-vertical staircase leading up to the simple, spectacular lodge.

Joe invited Bill Taylor and me to fish at Two Brooks for a few days in June 1994. The afternoon we arrived, the air was cool and the sky overcast. Because of staff rotation, we weren't scheduled to fish that evening. But Jerry Irvine, the chore boy, had just been promoted to guide, and he offered to accompany us if we wanted to get in a little dusk fishing near camp. We were to be his first sports.

By the time we got squared away and suited up, the afternoon was gone. It was one of those chilly, drizzly evenings that define salmon country. The scent of mist-cloaked pines suffused the damp air. A great silence lay over the river, bringing with it anticipation. It is on such evenings that salmon like to move.

We went upstream and cast without moving a fish. As nightfall approached, I stepped into Two Brooks's Home Pool, which is right below the lodge. I fished through using a size 6 Black and Blue double. About 20 minutes later, Bill and Jerry appeared, walking down the bank. I waded toward shore to meet them, my enthusiasm on the wane. Bill asked how far down I'd fished then encouraged me to go back out, because I hadn't fished through all the taking water. I did so, even though it was close to quitting time.

I'd just started fishing about 25 feet of line (including the 12-pound-test leader) when, at the end of a swing, I had a take so strong it yanked my arm down. I saw an enormous boil on the surface, and the next thing I knew my reel was shrieking while the fish bolted upstream. As it passed, the slack line audibly ripped through the water.

Stunned, I tried to reel up the slack, but within seconds the salmon was 80 yards *down*stream. The big fish leaped three, four times in succession. It was so dark I could barely see. I only knew that my fly line was knifing into the water and disappearing at an angle that seemed to have no relation to where the fish was jumping.

The salmon crossed back to the near side of the river and jumped twice more beside the bank. I don't know how quickly all this happened;

I only know that I was always a good four or five seconds behind events and unable to catch up.

I stumbled downstream and toward shore, reeling like mad, trying to keep a tight connection with the fish, which finally appeared to be slowing down.

By this time Jerry and Bill were well below me. I made my way down the gravel beach, slowly recovering line. The young guide stood up to his knees in the river, looking hard at the water. I finally recovered all my backing and began to spool fly line. Just as I got an idea of where the fish lay, sulking near the bottom, Jerry dipped the net and came up with the salmon. We carefully measured its length and girth before releasing it. According to the accepted mathematical formula published by the ASF and others, the fish weighed over 29 pounds—the largest salmon I've ever caught.

The most important element of this experience was sheer blind luck. I'd have never hooked that fish if Bill hadn't suggested I continue fishing. The salmon took on a short line, ideal but relatively rare for a wading angler. And I still don't know how such a large fish failed to break me off with its initial upstream burst; smaller fish have done so in similar circumstances.

I'm also amazed that the line held and the hook remained set when the fish took off downstream, exerting on the submerged line so much water pressure from such an unusual, indirect angle. The line's length and attitude prevented me from introducing slack by bowing to the fish in the traditional manner when it began to jump. I don't know how in all that frenzy the big fish never fell back onto the leader, severing it.

I'm still amazed that Jerry happened to take a position on the bank near the salmon, and that he could see the fish in the failing light and manage to net it on his first pass. The entire fight with this 29-pound fish lasted maybe six minutes. I've had 4-pound grilse resist for twice as long. Of course if the guide had missed the fish on his first pass, I could have been out there for at least another hour, my chances of landing the salmon diminishing as quickly as the light.

Ultimately I did only one thing right in the course of catching my largest-ever salmon. I didn't panic. I didn't panic passively, by becoming a paralyzed spectator, and I didn't panic actively, by trying to slow or stop the fish so that I could catch up. Salmon half that size can put you into equally helpless situations. But if you stay calm, you'll be surprised at how often things will turn out your way.

THE TAKE

The take is the most critical stage in catching a salmon, because it's the one over which you may—or may not—have the greatest control. This is especially true in dry-fly fishing, where it's critical to strike fish swiftly and firmly. But let's start with the wet fly.

THE WET FLY

In a classic take, a salmon sees a wet fly approaching and, in one uninterrupted motion, rises from its lie, pursues the fly a short distance, and seizes it as it turns to go back to its lie. The salmon's signature "pull"— that leisurely, heavy tug on the line for which salmon anglers live—is created less by the take than by the turn as the fish heads back for its lie with the fly in its jaws.

Fortunately the physics of a salmon taking and turning with a fly are ideal for ensuring a good hookup. Visualize a salmon taking a wet fly and you can see how and why the hook so often lodges in the ideal spot: the corner of the jaw, where the steel becomes firmly embedded in tough cartilage (see fig. 9-1).

That salmon take wet flies in so predictable and uniform a fashion is amazing; it also explains why the traditional "no-strike" method is virtually universal. As I mentioned in chapter 7, the British like to say "God Save the Queen" before sharply raising the rod. It's a worthy rule of thumb, but the truth is that by the time you raise your rod the hook is almost always well set. When you raise the rod after a take so that you can begin to play the fish, raise it with authority.

There is some disagreement about the best way to prepare for a take. After casting, some anglers like to fish with 2 or 3 feet of slack line held loosely between the fingers of the rod hand. When a salmon takes, they let the slack line slide out under light pressure from their fingers, then

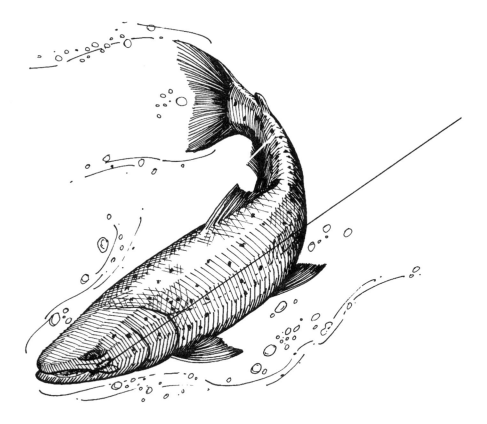

Figure 9-1. Hooking a salmon

firmly raise the rod once the slack runs out and the connection to the fish is established.

I prefer to fish directly off the reel—that is, after I cast the line, I'm left with no slack at all. However, I do keep the line between the index and middle fingers of my rod hand as I fish out the cast. Thus when a fish takes on a tight line, it pulls line off the reel, against the drag.

A botched hookup may be the most frustrating experience in wet-fly fishing. There are four common reasons for it, starting with getting excited and striking the fish the moment it shows itself rather than after it has taken the fly. I know some experienced anglers who insist on bucking conventional wisdom by striking salmon on the take, as if they were trout. These fellows have about the same success rate as the traditionalists—but then they don't strike as soon as they see a dorsal fin or blip of water. They only strike when the fish has securely taken the fly, so they never snatch the fly away from a willing salmon.

The three other common problems are all gear related. Sometimes a loop of line wraps around the rod's extension butt at the end of a cast. Line may hang up on the handles of certain reels. Then there's the problem of setting the drag too tight.

Fishing with a loop of line in hand solves most of these potential problems, because you manually form the loop at the end of each cast, clearing it from the rod butt and reel handles. The reel's drag setting isn't a factor, because the loop feeds out through your fingers, not off the reel. There are shortcomings, however. The loop introduces imprecision into the fishing of an exact length of line. The amount of pressure you put on the line also influences the take: Losing control of the loop increases the chances of making a bad hookup.

Water pressure on the line beyond the rod tip usually has much more influence on the take than the amount of finger pressure applied to the line, with one important exception. When a fish takes at the end of the swing in slack water, a lack of finger pressure can mean a poor hookup, since there isn't enough water pressure on the line to sink the hook well. But under such conditions, even a direct off-the-reel hookup can be weak.

When fishing off the reel, make sure after every cast that your line is clear, and adjust the drag to a minimal setting. A tight drag may result in the best hookups of all, particularly with large salmon. But grilse, small MSW salmon, and the occasional fish that takes delicately or oddly are usually hooked better using light resistance. A fish that takes savagely, especially a big one, can break you off on the take if it encounters too much resistance.

Although the wet-fly take is simple and a solid hookup easily achieved by doing nothing more than eventually raising your rod, it's helpful to be aware of the kinds of takes you're likely to get in different kinds of water and through different parts of your swing.

In general you'll get very solid hookups in fast water, because the line and water offer good resistance and the fish must grab the fly and turn quickly. Sometimes, however, a salmon will come up, grab the fly, and let it go when it feels strong resistance. Such a fish is probably better hooked with the slack-loop method—if you release the line as soon as the fish takes.

Takes and hookups become progressively less reliable as the water slows, because line tension lessens and in slower water fish needn't take with as much commitment. Usually, however, water swift enough to produce a tempting wet-fly swing is swift enough to provide a sure hookup.

The length of line you fish also influences the hookup. Most of us like to cast, and on days when our timing is good we particularly enjoy casting a long, straight line. But remember the old 45-at-45 rule (see chapter 7); beyond 45 feet, the chances of a solid hookup decrease in direct proportion to the amount of line you're fishing.

In either fast or slow water, you will at some point suddenly lose the feeling—as well as the advantage—of being connected to your fly. Often you'll see a bit of slack or an angle near the tip of your fly line as it approaches the end of the swing. When a salmon takes on a long line, the water provides all the resistance for the hookup, and a lot of line lying on the water means that this resistance is spongy at best, especially in slower water. There's nothing you can do about it; even if you strike with all your might, the energy will be dissipated before it reaches the fly. Always try to fish with the shortest line and tightest swing possible under the prevailing conditions.

In the typical 45-at-45 cast, your chance for a solid hookup is best near the top of the swing and diminishes through the swing. In other words, a fish hooked "broadside" to the angler is usually hooked best. This is because a line laid across the current provides more resistance and drags the hook into the corner of the salmon's mouth. In the fast water of a typical run, the odds of a good hookup change very little from the top to the bottom of the swing. But in slower water, or if the fly swings into slack water, the chance of a solid hookup may diminish considerably near the end of the swing—and drastically if you insist on fishing a long line.

A fly's action at the end of the swing, just as it swims around and comes to rest directly downstream from the angler—*on the dangle*—is often irresistible to salmon, particularly one that has followed the fly for a short distance. Fish that take on the dangle are sometimes hooked rather lightly in either the top or bottom of the lip rather than the jaw, and are thus lost more often than fish hooked across stream.

Most anglers agree that, with a typical wet-fly take, you need only raise the rod firmly to begin the fight. But I like to add one or two sharp pokes for insurance. I do this *after* I feel the fish is on and the rod has a healthy bend.

THE DRY FLY

With dry flies, you can throw all this geometry and physics out the window. Given the regal leisure with which a salmon takes a wet fly, refusing to let go despite the line's drag, it's astonishing that the same fish may explode on a dry fly and quickly eject it before you can strike. It's just another one of those behavioral mysteries.

Even if the hook doesn't prick it, a salmon struck late usually won't return for a fly. Your chances of raising the fish again are a little better if you strike too early and pull the fly away before the salmon can grab it. With salmon on the dry fly the golden rule is: Strike immediately but not prematurely.

Easier said than done.

The sight of a salmon coming to a dry fly can unnerve even a veteran angler. It may plow across the current, head above the water and mouth agape, or well up from its lie majestically and inexorably, taking ages to reach the fly. My favorite take occurs in deep water. Suddenly you see the salmon's white belly undulating upward like a serpent, then *the take*. In any event, most salmon riseforms give you plenty of time to snatch your fly away from the fish.

The trick to a good dry-fly hookup is to react to the fly rather than to the fish. Don't strike because you see the white inside of the salmon's mouth, or because its back is halfway out of the water. Watch your fly, and strike the moment it disappears. This all transpires in the blink of an eye: One moment you're astonished at the sight of a salmon moving for your fly, and the next you either have the fish on or the fly is hung up in a bough behind you.

Before fishing a dry fly, you'll need to adjust your reel's drag to a moderate setting suitable for fighting fish. With a wet fly, you want minimal drag so that the fish can hook itself well. But dry-fly takes are more explosive, and some drag helps ensure a solid hookup. Because the fish often reacts immediately to the hook, setting the drag also prepares you for the fight as soon as the take occurs.

Your strike itself must be sharp and hard; jerk down with your line hand as you snap the rod up. If you hold the line lightly between the fingers of your rod hand, the line may slip as you strike, making it difficult to sink the hook into a large salmon's tough jaw.

HOOKED UP

You're hooked up, and now the fun begins. Although the experience I had with the 29-pounder at Two Brooks may suggest the opposite, most salmon that take a wet fly react slowly to being hooked. Typically a fish will swim back to its lie and slowly recognize that things aren't quite right. Often its next reaction is to swim slowly upstream. Although we're talking about only six or eight seconds here, it is enough time for you to clear slack line, quickly check your drag, and—most important—get mentally squared away for the battle to come.

Atlantic salmon typically fight in a stately manner, making a series of long, well-modulated runs rather than frenzied, zigzagging sprints. They tend to bore powerfully upstream, slowly shaking their heads from side to side, or to race downstream. They rarely make for bankside deadfalls or riverbed snags. They often leap with heart-rending grace rather than convulsive abandon. Fortunately these traits play into the hands of the angler, who needs all the help he can get.

However, note that salmon hooked on a dry fly are more likely to become explosive the moment you strike. This is another reason for having your drag set at a moderate level when fishing the dry fly.

Upon hooking up, get tight on the fish, with no slack in your line. Adjust your drag for light to medium resistance for this initial and often critical portion of the fight. Keep your rod high and, without rushing, head for shore and a place where you can fight the fish on firm footing in shallow water, preferably free from brush or debris. This may mean going one way while the fish goes the other. Don't worry about this; if the fish is in the midst of a frenzied action, though, wait until the outburst is over.

Once you're near shore and squared away, crank down your drag a little more—but not too much. Under most conditions, a 12-pound-test

A hard-fighting salmon on a Gaspe river (Photo: Val Atkinson)

leader will hold any salmon you're likely to hook. At the same time, however, any MSW salmon can snap a 12-pound leader with a sudden, explosive move. Stick with a drag setting that provides plenty of cushion until you get an inkling of the fish's character and how it will fight.

After the fish is on, your best allies are confidence in your equipment (including your knots) and a good sense of what the fish may do in the specific environment. The first issue is under your control, but the second is a little more complicated. Before fishing a pool, it's always a good idea to assess it from the viewpoint of a fighting fish. If you forget to do this, you'll have to take a quick read at the most awkward time— shortly after hooking up.

On some rivers, or parts of rivers, salmon have limited options. The Miramichi is broad and well tempered, with long, relatively shallow and even-bottomed pools—an ideal river for playing and landing salmon, a river where you can let a fish go where it will, knowing there are few elements it can use against you.

By contrast a Miramichi tributary, the Little Southwest, is a wild, mountain river strewn with sharp boulders and heavy riffles between pools. If you hook a big salmon on the Little Southwest and it decides to run downstream, you're in for one rough ride.

Here are some general rules to keep in mind:

- Fish rarely run upstream for any significant distance, except in slow water. Those that do are usually easy to control and subdue.
- Salmon hooked at the head of a pool never run up into heavy water. Most fish hooked at the head of a pool turn and quickly go back downstream, even if they start upstream after being hooked.
- Fish hooked in smooth tailouts above heavy whitewater can be big trouble, because they often turn and immediately head downstream. When this happens, downstream boulders, snags, or impassable obstructions on the bank can spell disaster.
- Fish hooked at the head of a long pool usually stay in the pool.
- Fish hooked in swift runs almost always run downstream to the first proper pool, where they often stay for the duration of the fight.

Once you're positioned on the bank, you have two goals while fighting the fish: getting across and slightly downstream of it, and keeping it from leaving the pool if there's heavy water below. The secret to tiring a salmon quickly is keeping it under constant pressure from the side. If a salmon is allowed to face directly upstream, it can rest and draw oxygen—fuel for the fight—from the water. The harder the fish must work to keep that direct upstream position, the more quickly it will yield.

Always keep pressure on the fish, except when it jumps; then, drop your rod and bow deeply at the waist, creating enough slack to prevent the fish from falling back onto a taut leader and snapping it. How much pressure to apply is dictated both by what the fish is doing and by the implications of letting the fish have its way. If it's heading for a rough, rocky chute below the pool, and a steep bank or obstacles makes following it hazardous, you'll have to apply a lot of pressure even at the risk of losing it. But if the fish is just busting up a big pool, let it go and enjoy the ride. Fish that go berserk eventually have to rest, giving you time to get into a better position.

Although the superior position for tiring a fish is across and slightly downstream from it, salmon will seldom yield you that advantage until relatively late in a struggle. In many cases, the nature of the river and bank will also prohibit you from taking that ideal position. Because salmon are on a mission to spawn, they are in general terms upstream minded. But when a hooked fish realizes the gravity of the situation, its flight instinct takes over and compels it to run hard and fast along the path of least resistance—downstream.

On its initial run a salmon will often go far downstream, leaving you with so much line and backing out that you won't even be sure that you're still hooked up. Always try to bring the fish back up to you instead of chasing it downstream, because the latter can so easily degenerate into a futile game of leapfrog. It's much better to hold your ground when possible. On a broad river with an even, moderate flow, you can simultaneously stay tight to the distant fish, recover line, and move downstream. Your immediate goal is to get close enough to the fish to put pressure on it.

But on a very swift river, or if the fish has left a distinct pool, a salmon just 100 feet away can be impossible to bring back upstream. In these cases you must go downstream—although not necessarily below the fish—until you're once again in a position to put pressure on it. Hooked salmon can see or sense you trying to get below them, and they almost inevitably counter by beating you to the punch. If you're too hellbent on getting below a fish, you may even force it to leave the pool.

Because salmon are upstream minded, many of them are reluctant to leave a pool, particularly if the water immediately below it—which they so recently traveled through—is very rough. You can capitalize on this critical salmon error. Stay slightly upstream of the fish and apply pressure to it, and you may coax it back up into the pool. Often you can "walk" the fish upstream; in these cases it responds like a reluctant dog on a leash, following you upstream as you walk on the bank.

Always keep in mind that the closer you are to the fish, the more pressure you can put on it. The standard way to apply pressure and gain ground is to *pump* the fish—alternately raising and lowering your rod, recovering line each time you lower it.

Typically, an angler strives to hold the rod straight up, at a 40- to 90-degree angle to the water, with the fighting butt resting against his midsection. I find it's much more effective to change the angle of the rod frequently, however, putting pressure on the fish from a variety of angles. When I really want to move a fish I put my left hand (I'm a lefty) below the first guide, my right hand on the fighting butt; with the rod parallel to the water, I turn my entire torso slowly. Side pressure is more effective than vertical. Changing the angle of the rod keeps a salmon off balance and puts pressure on it from different directions. The goal of the pressure is always to turn the head of the fish out of the straight-upstream position.

Of course, accomplishing this also means that you're almost forcing the fish to turn and head downstream, which again raises the threat of the salmon leaving the pool. If it does, and it gets into heavy water, just follow it downstream to the next viable place to fight—without breaking your rod or your neck. You can do nothing to control a big salmon wallowing and rolling downstream through whitewater. Just reduce your drag to a minimal setting, hold your rod high overhead, and slowly make your way downstream. Keep an eye out for places where your line might hang up; you won't want to head back upstream to free it later. Eventually you'll either recover all of your line with no fish attached, or you'll find your salmon in the next pool down, still hooked and awaiting the next stage of the battle.

The middle stage of the fight often becomes a tug-of-war interspersed with shorter runs and a few jumps. You can tighten up on your drag now, because the fish is less likely to break you off with a power move, and because the harder it must work to hold or change position, the more quickly it will tire. Ultimately the combination of fatigue and the salmon's desperate desire to maintain its requisite straight-upstream position will allow you to control its movements with very little pressure.

If you apply sufficient cross-stream pressure without giving a fish opportunities for rest and recovery, you'll see that Lee Wulff was right: A salmon well fought is landed at the rate of one minute per pound. In other words, you should be able to land a 12-pound salmon in about 12 minutes.

END GAME

The final stages of a battle can be as tricky as the beginning. When you feel a fish is ready for the net, back way off your drag and rely on manual pressure. This is where an exposed-spool rim suitable for palming comes in handy. The first time a fish sees the net or a human captor, it often recovers and takes off on yet another run. If you have trouble netting or tailing it at this point, it may make two or three more runs, although they usually diminish in length and power. The important thing is to remain patient. Trying to force the struggle to a conclusion with a wild swipe of the net or by grabbing the line is an invitation to disaster.

The best device for landing a fish is a deep, long-handled net with a soft knotless mesh bag, particularly if you have someone along to serve as netsman. A net is awkward to carry and always seems to be far away when you need it, but it's also the quickest and least damaging way to land and release a salmon.

Safely in the net (Photo: Val Atkinson)

Near the end of the fight, the netsman should take up position at least 6 feet directly downstream from the angler, being careful not to wade out so far that the fish could run downstream between them, possibly tangling the line in the net—or around the netsman's legs. The net should be kept under the water; nothing terrifies a fish more than a net suddenly plunged into the water below or beside it. With the net below the surface, the netsman can smoothly and easily slide it into position from behind and under the fish.

If your netsman is in a good position below you and the water is clear enough for him to see the fish, try to steer the salmon to the net. The netsman should let the fish swim or drift into the net, moving it as little as possible and resisting the temptation to swipe.

If you're wade fishing alone, your net is invariably back on the bank back where you started fishing. By the time you hook a salmon, you're so far downstream that going back for the net is out of the question. On public water, other nearby anglers with nets are usually ready and eager to help. If not, solo anglers usually beach or tail their fish.

Beaching is an easy way to land a salmon, but it should be practiced on one you intend to release. To beach a fish properly, you need a relatively flat, smooth beach of gravel or sand. When the fish is tired, hold your rod high and slowly step back up the beach, gently dragging the fish up onto the shore. When it's far enough up that it can't flip back in with one flop, quickly pull a few feet of line off your reel, lay your rod down, and go get your fish.

Tailing is a trickier exercise, but many experienced catch-and-release anglers prefer it—and for a solo angler trying to land a fish while standing knee deep in flowing water, it's the *only* effective technique. Tailing means grabbing a salmon by the fleshy narrow "wrist" just above its tail, a move that immobilizes it. Though tailing is common, hoisting a fish clear of the water with its head dangling down may injure a salmon's internal organs. You can tail an MSW salmon and hold it parallel to the surface with surprising authority. Grilse, which have a less pronounced wrist, can be difficult to hand-tail.

Before tailing a salmon it's vital to tire it completely, though not necessarily exhaust it. Begin by moving your rod upstream and behind you. Sometimes it helps to hold the rod by the shaft, with the cork grip resting against your forearm or waist as you swing the fish close to your body and grasp its tail. Some anglers find that using a dry bandanna, handkerchief, or glove gives them additional security. Once you've grasped the tail, hold the fish close to your body. Strip a few feet of line off the reel and tuck the rod under your arm so that you can use both hands to hold the fish and remove the hook.

The mechanical tailer is a handy but potentially harmful little device that's rarely used on this side of the Atlantic. The most common type is about 2 feet long and works like a simple snare. You just slide a loop of cable over the fish's tail while it's in the water, then snatch the tailer upward to draw the loop tight. The more pressure you put on the loop, the tighter it holds the fish. The trouble with the typical commercial tailer is that it has a fairly long shaft, it must be "loaded" to work properly, and the steel cable is harmful to the fish. All in all, you're better off with a net.

The key components in catching and releasing salmon successfully are playing and landing the fish swiftly and firmly—meaning with purpose, skill, authority, and confidence, and with as few false passes and blown opportunities as possible. If you intend to release a salmon, don't drag it up on a rough stone bank. And don't play a fish to near exhaustion, botch repeated attempts to hand-tail it, then drag it over to shore and put it through a 20-minute photo session.

The critical element in the survival of a released fish is keeping it in the water as much as possible while you remove the hook, take pictures, or simply admire the gorgeous creature. Barbless hooks are certainly easier on fish, but an MSW salmon has a large, tough mouth, and hook-related mortality is relatively low.

Ensure that every salmon you release is in good shape when you let it go, even those you fought and landed quickly and easily. After removing the hook, hold the wrist of the salmon's tail lightly but firmly with one hand, and, with the fish facing directly upstream, in a place where water can flow freely through its mouth and gills, support its belly with the other. Stroke the belly, allowing the fish to "burp" up any air it ingested during landing. Hold the tail just tightly enough that the fish can't escape without a pronounced flick of its tail. If you did everything right, the salmon will have no trouble doing just that.

CHAPTER 10

Tips for Difficult Salmon

Certain experiences not only teach us a great deal but also provide the enthusiasm and confidence we need to advance to the next plateau as anglers. I had one of these experiences on a hot day in late July almost 20 years ago, during low water on the Ste. Jean River. I was relatively new to salmon angling, and the few fish I'd caught were hooked while I blind cast with a wet fly.

I started this day by fishing a stretch of the lower river that my companions, Chris von Strasser and Bill George, had leased for a few days from Pat Baker, who was too busy running a motorcyclists' tavern in the town of Gaspe to care much about fishing the salmon water he owned. The pool was dead, so I went exploring upstream. About ½ mile up I came to a pool few people bothered to fish.

It was a long run below the high bank along a dirt road. From the roadside I spotted two salmon lying side by side in about 4 feet of water in the heart of the run. I ran about 50 feet upstream and, scampering down the bank, stripped out line like a madman. I began fishing through the pool with my wet fly, expecting a take at any moment.

When nothing happened, and I was sure I'd covered the salmon, I had the good sense to calm down, wade out of the river, and go back up on the high bank. I located the fish again, and this time headed right down to the water's edge and built a small pile of stones to mark their approximate location. I went back upstream and fished over the salmon again with a different fly, my cairn giving me a feeling of certitude and purpose.

I kept working the salmon, trying various wet flies and occasionally climbing the bank to make sure the fish were still there. I pounded those fish for about an hour without seeing even a swirl of interest. It was approaching high noon, the day was developing into another scorcher, and my chances of hooking a fish were growing slimmer. I'd read Lee Wulff's book on salmon fishing and remembered that he used a special knot to make a fly wake or sputter across the surface in a way that sometimes tempts reluctant salmon. Called the *riffling* or *Portland Creek hitch,* it's just a half hitch slipped over the fly's head so that the leader is perpendicular to the hook shank (see fig. 10-1). This causes the fly to ride up in the surface film, making a very visible commotion.

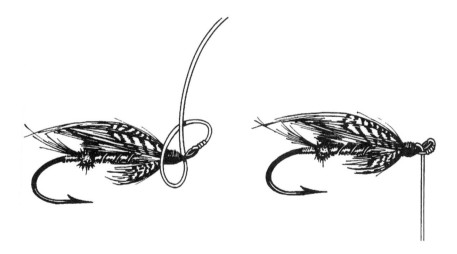

Figure 10-1. Riffling hitch

So I tied on a Miramichi Butterfly and added a riffling hitch at the head. As I began to fish down, Chris and his father, Rudy, pulled up on the road to collect me for lunch. From the river, I gave them a quick synopsis and asked them to wait while I made my last, desperate effort. As I entered the hot zone, Chris suddenly shouted, "Here he comes, here he comes!" The next thing I knew, a salmon's large head poked through the surface—and it had the fly. I landed that fish and basked in my great—if temporary—feeling of expertise. I'd caught a salmon under very difficult conditions: at high noon, using a special technique, in front of my fishing companions. It doesn't get much better than that.

It was four years before I caught another salmon using the riffling hitch.

Still, by now I've caught a number of fish using that technique, one of a limited number of variations on the traditional down-and-across wet-fly theme. Although discussing special techniques in great detail is beyond the scope of this book, I'd like to pass along a few tips and strategies to keep in mind when the fish are in the river but the fishing is slow.

INDIFFERENT FISH

The longer you fish for salmon, the more you realize that the vast majority of those you cover under all but the most favorable conditions are not automatically predisposed to take a fly. Three components influence the taking behavior of salmon: the *individual fish, the general water and weather conditions,* and *the specific daily conditions.* If the fish are relatively fresh and the general conditions are good, the specific daily conditions are usually irrelevant. But if the fishing has been slow because the fish are pooled up, and the water is low and relatively warm, specific daily conditions can become very important.

At such times early mornings and late evenings are the best times to fish. A high, bright sun is usually the kiss of death. I don't know if intense sunlight blinds the fish, or if it makes flies look different and less appealing, or if the degree of light simply shuts down a salmon's curiosity or its willingness to move. But bright sunlight does create difficult—though not impossible—conditions. If you are fishing low water under a bright sun, try to fish from the *weak* side—the side from which a fish must turn away from the sun rather than toward it to take the fly.

The wild card in salmon taking behavior is the fish itself. As a species, and even on an individual basis, salmon are moody, unpredictable, and enigmatic. There are times when plenty of seemingly fresh fish are in a river, both the general and specific conditions are good, and still the salmon won't take. It's as if a sorcerer has cast some kind of spell over them—or over you. This doesn't happen often, but it happens. So imagine how your problems are compounded when the conditions *aren't* favorable.

One of the main reasons for salmon's unpredictability is the behavioral effects of the biological law that causes them gradually to lose interest in everything but spawning once they enter fresh water. I feel that during dog days, or even during a long stretch of similar days, salmon slip into something like a semicomatose state. But although the salmon's feeding or killing instincts grow dim in rivers, even stale fish are apt to take flies after a dramatic change in water level "freshens" the river and gets them moving. Perhaps the exercise and change of scenery once again put their senses on alert.

Salmon are indifferent to flies more often than they're interested, and for more of the total time that they spend in rivers. Unless the fish are very active and in full taking mode, their initial reaction to a well-presented fly is often their only reaction. A fly's novelty quickly wears off for all but the freshest salmon. That's why it's critical to give the fish the best first look at a fly, and why it's so important to keep searching for the "sacred inch" when using the dry fly.

Invariably you will find yourself someday on a pool whose salmon show absolutely no interest in your fly. One of the most striking techniques described in the salmon literature is *stoning*, wherein an angler throws large stones into a pool containing apparently comatose salmon in order to "stir them up." Sometimes this actually works, as does the related technique of buzzing through the heart of a pool with a motorized boat. Thankfully, neither strategy works often enough to merit a place in an angler's basic repertoire. These are purely desperation measures.

But there are other, more subtle ways to stir up fish and get them interested in flies. Showing the salmon something new and different is always a good idea when the fishing is slow, even if that means skittering a huge dry fly through a low-water pool when all the other anglers in the Rotation (see chapter 11) are using tiny wet flies—or vice versa. The most novel practice may be fishing a pool backward—that is, fishing it from the bottom up, taking a step upstream instead of downstream after each cast. For obvious logistical reasons this can be a real pain, but it has worked.

When you want or need to depart from the traditional style of wet-fly fishing, there are four overlapping factors to consider, individually or in combination: *your flies, your techniques, the water,* and *the fish.* There are fewer variations on traditional dry-fly fishing, partly because there are fewer options in presentation and partly because most of the seemingly unconventional presentations (such as skittering) are already part of the dry-fly tradition.

In the summer of 1995, I fished the public water of the Bonaventure out of Glen LeGrand's camp with Richard Franklin and a field officer for the Atlantic Salmon Federation, Lewis Hinks. The fishing was slow because of low water, but a few Quebecois fishermen sitting beside a pool called Little Black's told us that a handful of salmon were holding near the bottom in the swift, deep run at the head of the pool. They had seen the fish with a "viewing box," a kind of reverse periscope that some salmon anglers carry. In clear water, you can spot salmon at surprisingly great distances with this instrument (see chapter 11).

I went down to the tail of the pool to fish dry flies over some visible salmon there, and Lewis went up to fish the run. After Louis made a few unsuccessful passes, our guide, Glen Hayes, had an idea. He knew that fishing small flies in the run near the surface was futile, and fishing with weighted flies is illegal. So Glen found an enormous streamer fly—a Magog Smelt—in his kit and advised Lewis to fish it as deep as he could, using every casting and mending technique he knew. On his first pass through the pool, Lewis hooked, landed, and released a 10-pound salmon.

This is a clear example of how fly selection *can* make a difference—in this case, a logical, obvious one.

Fishing down at the salmon's level is a good strategy anytime fish are reluctant to rise to a fly. It also raises thorny ethical problems (see chapter 11); still, some of the most revered, traditional techniques that I'll discuss shortly are effective precisely because they manage to put the fly closer to the salmon.

One of the most overlooked methods of salmon angling is the use of nymphs in low, clear water. This can be exciting and challenging sight fishing, comparable with flats fishing for bonefish. If you're interested in nymphs, check out the simple and elegant salmon series created by pioneering fly tyer Charles DeFeo.

Don't be afraid to try unique or untraditional flies such as Glo-Bugs (yarn imitations of salmon eggs), large streamers (properly speaking, the classic Mickey Finn and Muddler Minnow aren't salmon flies, but they are very attractive to salmon), Matukas, Woolly Buggers, and so on. But always be aware that in low water, most of the time, smaller really is better.

RIFFLING HITCH

There are three special techniques you should be prepared to use under difficult conditions. The most common is the aforementioned riffling hitch. This technique originated on Newfoundland's Portland Creek, where the salmon often preferred a waking fly to one swimming in the

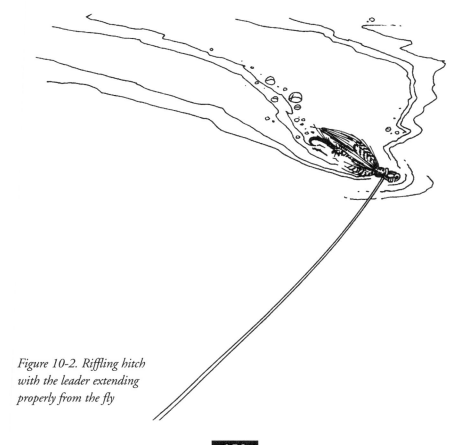

Figure 10-2. Riffling hitch with the leader extending properly from the fly

more sedate, traditional way. A few points about tying and fishing the hitch: Make sure that the half hitch seats with a good bite right behind the hook eye, with the leader perpendicular to the hook shank and on your side of the fly. That is, if you're going to fish downstream along the right bank, the leader should extend from the fly toward the right bank (see fig. 10-2). If you put the hitch on the wrong side of the fly, it will just tumble and splash as if it's been fouled.

By design, the riffling hitch slips over the hook eye and comes undone when a certain amount of tension is put on the fly and leader. Ideally this only happens after a salmon takes, leaving you with a strong, conventional knot and a straight connection to the fish. In heavy or very fast water, however, a single hitch can come undone on its own with every cast. For this reason, some anglers like to slip two half hitches over the fly. Most of the time it's easy to tell when your hitch has come undone, because the fly no longer makes its characteristic wake.

Fish a hitched fly just as you would an ordinary wet fly, observing the 45-at-45 rule. Its unique action depends heavily on water tension, so slack line can kill the effect. In fast water the hitched fly burbles and spurts along. As the water slows, the fly begins to skate along on the surface. If the water slows so much that the fly no longer makes a wake, don't use the hitch.

I like to use the riffling hitch at the extremes of surface conditions—in very smooth, glassy water where the fly leaves a conspicuous wake, or in water where bottom structure or other elements create upwellings, boils, and other current variations. In the latter kind of water, a regular drift is merely inconsistent, while a hitched fly acts so zany that it often triggers a reaction take. One of my most memorable salmon savagely attacked a riffle-hitched Muddler on a turbulent pool on the Matane. Its unique deer hair head makes the Muddler especially enticing as a hitched fly. I also like to hitch the Butterfly.

GREASED LINE

The greased line technique is the subject of a wonderful little volume called *Greased Line Fishing for Atlantic Salmon* by Jock Scott (a playful pseudonym for the British angler and author Donald G. H. Rudd). The book was published in England in 1935 (and reprinted by Andre Deutsch in London, 1985)—a time when most salmon fishing was done with sunken lines and large flies. Essentially, greased line fishing is a dead-drift presentation of light flies with a floating line from directly across stream (see fig. 10-3). As the book's title implies, the strategy was developed back in the days when the only way to make fly lines float was through the liberal application of greasy flotant.

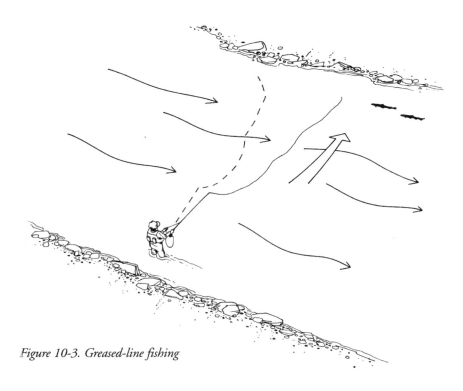

Figure 10-3. Greased-line fishing

Here's a real-world situation where trying the greased-line technique makes sense. You're wade fishing and spot a salmon lying near the far bank in the smooth tailout of a long pool. The pool's depth, its width, or a physical obstruction on the bank prevents your making anything like a 45-degree cast. The current near the fish is slow, and crossing the river and fishing from the far bank won't work because of the nature of the shoreline and the slow current.

Using the greased-line technique, you can cast across stream and dead-drift a wet fly so that it rides perpendicular to the current over the salmon. Although these days it's no longer necessary to grease your line to keep the fly near the surface, dressing your leader to within a few inches of your fly can be very helpful. It's most important, however, to choose a wet fly that lends itself to greased-line fishing. A sparse hairwing Silver Rat sinks like a stone in slow water, but a Spey-style fly such as the Gold Rioch, with its woolly body, long, soft hackles, and light, delicate featherwing, will hang in the water in a very enticing way. You can dress the fly with flotant to keep it riding even higher.

Greased-line fishing was a tentative step toward a technique the tradition-bound British never cultivated: dry-fly fishing. Most of the situations that prompt a savvy British angler to choose the greased-line technique are tailor-made for dry-fly fishing. Nevertheless, I have hooked fish using the greased-line technique after they refused dry flies. And when the air and water are too cold to score consistently with dry flies, the greased-line technique is the next best thing.

THOMPSON'S PATENT

The Patent, or Thompson's Patent, is another intriguing technique, and by far the most radical of the alternate strategies. It was pioneered and first described in print in 1934 by Colonel Lewis S. Thompson. Richard Hunt, one of Thompson's regular fishing companions and a fellow member of the Anglers' Club of New York, also described the method in detail in his terrific little book *Salmon in Low Water*.

The Patent was born when Thompson made a sloppy upstream cast just to mark time after a salmon rose near him. As the enormous 5/0 Red Abbey dead-drifted downstream, its hackles and wing suspended and fluffed out in the water, a great salmon that no one previously had been able to raise engulfed the fly. Basically the Patent is a technique for dead-drifting wet flies, and it goes against almost every element in salmon fishing tradition. It's easiest to fish the Patent upstream, but Thompson ended up fishing it downstream as well, stopping the rod before the end of the cast to introduce slack, which allowed the fly to drift freely. Thompson made it quite clear that it didn't really matter where you cast; the idea was to cover as much water as possible by allowing the fly to go where it would.

Hairy flies with body components that pulse or undulate work best with the Patent. Because the flies float freely, salmon should be struck immediately, just like trout that take nymphs fished upstream. I've experimented with the Patent now and then, but haven't enjoyed much success.

SPEED CONTROL

At various points in this book I've discussed the importance—to both salmon and angler—of fly speed and current speed. Unfortunately salmon aren't always found where currents automatically create the perfect fly speed—one that leaves the angler with no tougher a task than to cast the fly and let it swing around. In high water, for instance, large areas of relatively slow water that ordinarily wouldn't hold salmon may provide viable resting lies. In these conditions, the major problem is finding fish.

Low water, however, concentrates fish in the best pools and drastically limits their options. Finding salmon becomes easy, especially on clear, low rivers. But these same conditions may make the fish less apt to take, as well as reduce the amount of water that will naturally provide the right, brisk fly speed. This is another powerful argument for concentrating on the dry fly during low water. Salmon will rise to a dry fly in water so slow that fishing a wet fly in it is a complete waste of time.

Sometimes, however, manual manipulation of the line can increase your chances of raising a fish with a wet fly. If the current is too slow to yield a good swing, experiment with stripping your line by hand to get the fly moving more quickly. Even under moderate to high water levels, parts of some pools may be covered more effectively by stripping the fly. You can always control how much movement you impart. Stripping the fly can be particularly effective in tailouts, because in low water the river often doesn't speed up until the very lip of a pool.

There is another good way to increase fly speed without manually manipulating the line. Instead of following the line all the way around through the swing, stop your rod and draw it slightly upstream near the end of the swing. This automatically speeds the fly, although not nearly as much as manual manipulation.

There are other conditions under which you'll want to slow your fly to enhance efficiency or tempt contrary fish. Salmon sometimes hold in very swift water, where a typical cast and swing pass the fly much too quickly and too high above them. This is a common problem in high water, but it exists in an even more challenging form during low water. On rivers susceptible to high temperatures, already lethargic salmon often seek comfort in the only place they can find cool, well-oxygenated water—at the very bottom of deep, fast runs, especially ones that begin with whitewater.

The simple upstream *reach-mend* (see fig. 10-4)—an ordinary mend finished with an exaggerated upstream and forward reach of the arm—is a good tool for slowing your fly. The reach-mend allows the fly and line

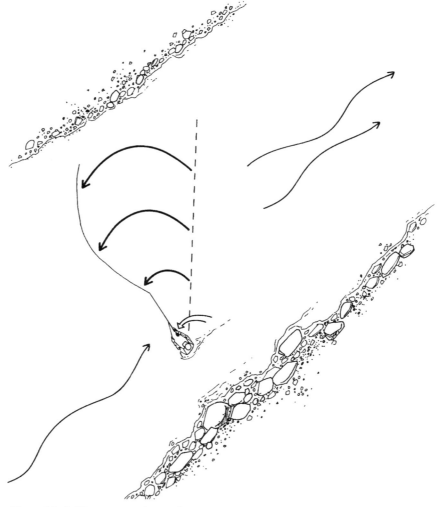

Figure 10-4. Upstream reach-mend

to make a fairly long dead drift that in swift water isn't really a dead drift at all, but a leisurely swing similar to the one produced by the greased-line method. When the line comes tight, it speeds the fly in a way that can be very attractive if it happens to occur over a salmon.

At this point, about a third of the way into the swing, you can often throw another mend into the line to keep it moving slowly and to keep the fly submerged. This is where a long rod (10 feet or more) can be very helpful. Generally you won't have enough time to make more than two mends in swift water, but if you time them properly, they will slow the fly significantly and sometimes goad dour fish into taking.

By and large, techniques for speeding or slowing a fly should be practiced on a pool-by-pool basis; the specific conditions will suggest just how fast to strip a fly or how large a mend to throw into the line.

SHORT TAKES

False or short takes are just a couple more of the sport's mysteries. A salmon that wants a fly has absolutely no trouble catching it, even in the swiftest and darkest of waters. Yet at times salmon will come to a fly in an astonishing variety of ways and never take it. I've known visible fish to move for a dry fly a dozen or more times without once making the critical decision to open their mouths. Sometimes I'm sure I just didn't find the sacred inch. But at many other times I think the fish was content to chase or examine the fly with no intention of catching, killing, or eating it. These false-takers can often be worked and induced to take, using the techniques described in chapter 8.

The short take is even more puzzling. At times a take will be a feeble, half-hearted tug that just peters out before you come tight on the fish. This almost always occurs in medium to slow water. I haven't actually seen a salmon taking short, but from the feel of it I assume that the tugger rises indolently and takes the fly so gently that it pulls free as the line begins to tighten—almost as if the fish wants merely to crush the fly. And even very large salmon are able and sometimes determined to grab a small fly by the very tip of the wing.

The first time I experienced a short take I was fishing with Lorne Irvine, the camp manager for Joe and Edgar Cullman at Runnymede on

Jim Emery's fly box (Photo: Richard Franklin)

the Restigouche River. Lorne had me strip in immediately, then he trimmed back the wing on the size 6 Rusty Rat double. I shortened up a tiny bit and cast, and the 25-pounder took solidly.

Although trimming back the wing after a short take from a tugger works, I prefer to change to a low-water single dressing in the same pattern—regardless of water conditions. Low-water single dressings are lethal on tuggers and other short-taking fish, because there's so much shank and hook behind the fly body.

There's no real pattern with other short takes; you just feel a tug too solid or long to be a parr or trout. In fast water, the fly seems to pull out of the mouths of some fish as they turn, usually because of the way they take it. But sometimes a fish merely wants to nip at the fly. The most effective technique for hooking such a fish is to shorten up slightly (about 6 inches) and make a mend, or a bigger mend, in your next cast.

Executed properly, this will slow the fly and cause it to swim just a little deeper. Just remember to give the fish you rolled sufficient time to return and settle into its lie before you try again.

The most bizarre short take is the aggressive one—a hard, fast, almost electric jolt, after which the line goes dead. It's difficult to imagine how a salmon can rap a fly hard enough to send a jolt through the line yet not get hooked. I think jolters miss because they're too impetuous, or because they nail the fly without really wanting to engulf it. The good news for the angler is that, more than any other idiosyncratic taker, the jolter is almost always suicidal. There's a good chance it will come back on the very next cast to take the fly more solidly.

Jim Emery and I were fishing one of our favorite pools on the Matapedia a few years ago when I had a classic experience with a jolter. I was fishing about 25 feet of line when I felt two sharp jolts. A moment later the salmon took so hard that my drag screamed. After a split second the fish jumped twice just a few feet away, heading upstream, and before I knew it my 12-pound-test leader was cleanly severed. I don't believe the salmon fell on it; it probably broke from the sheer strain applied by that explosive fish. Jolters are often that way.

Tuggers, nippers, and jolters. These don't represent typical salmon or typical taking behavior, but you should be prepared to encounter them.

CHAPTER 11

Etiquette and Ethics

Etiquette is the art of getting along with others. *Ethics* is the art of getting along with yourself as well as others. This is as true of life on a salmon river as anywhere else, although a breach of etiquette while fishing usually elicits a much stronger reaction from those around you than does burping in a restaurant.

This is because on the river, etiquette is uncomplicated and not at all concerned with nuances. It's a bare-bones code for fairly sharing the resource.

Unlike trout streams, where fish are usually distributed pretty evenly through the acceptable habitat, salmon rivers have long areas through which fish merely pass en route to preferred runs and pools. The quality of this limited habitat varies and also changes with water levels. This can create stiff competition for limited water.

When my friends Chris von Strasser and Bill George first began knocking around the Gaspe Peninsula many years ago, they once got tired of exploring and decided to fish the historic Forks Pool, where the the Matapedia and the Causapscal meet to form the main river. This is one of the classic pools, and it's fished hard by many anglers every day of salmon season. Bill and Chris were determined to be the first ones through, so they decided to be on the bank at the head of the pool at 4 A.M., almost two hours before legal fishing time.

That morning they made their way to the pool by flashlight through the darkness. When they turned off their flashlights and their eyes adjusted to the dark, they saw the glowing red tips of a half-dozen cigarettes. About eight fishermen had already established their right to fish through the pool first, as dictated by the Sumerian Code of salmon fishing: the *Rotation.* This is a standard feature on every stretch of public salmon water where more than one angler wants to fish.

In the Rotation, anglers form an informal waiting line depending on their order of arrival at the pool. The sport who was first to arrive— Angler 1—gets to fish through the pool first. He enters at the top of the pool (the beginning and end of the taking water is pretty easy to figure out on a pool popular enough to be fished in Rotation) and fishes down at a "reasonable" step-cast-step pace. Once he has proceeded about 20 yards downstream, Angler 2 gets in at the top of the taking water.

If Angler 1 happens to roll a fish, he can work it with a few casts and then change flies (one fly change is the norm, although many anglers manage two before the others begin grousing). But after trying about a dozen casts, Angler 1 must move on. When Angler 2 gets 20 yards down, Angler 3 enters at the top, and so on. With enough anglers, the Rotation becomes a kind of conga line.

When Angler 1 finishes his turn, he can go up and start again—provided no one is ahead of him, waiting his turn. Most of the time, even when there is a wait it isn't very long. But on some pools during crowded days, you may have to wait for an hour or more before it's your turn to fish through again. The social aspects of the Rotation system lend a certain charm to the drill. Most pools have benches or picnic tables where the waiting anglers tell lies, show off new flies, and tell more lies. And pools that develop Rotations *always* hold fish, so you know you'll put your fly over a salmon when your turn does come.

Unfortunately there are enough frustrating things about fishing in a Rotation to keep me from doing it very often. First of all, Rotations usually begin much too early in the morning. On private water, nobody begins fishing until the sun is well up, at around 8:30. This isn't entirely because laziness is a luxury the privileged can afford: Salmon generally take best after settling into their lies, and the fish are often still moving in the early morning. When the sun first hits the water is the best time to fish; the other good time is after the sun has gone off the water in the evening. The worst time is the long period when the sun is directly overhead, usually from about 11:30 A.M. until 4:30 P.M.

Anglers in a Rotation generally begin fishing as soon as it's legal to do so (usually this is about an hour before sunrise), and they continue pounding the water throughout the day. Obviously, fish still take under these circumstances, but most of the time it's just too much of a rat race for me. My other problems with a Rotation are that I like to experiment too much to enjoy such a strict routine, and that I hate to fish—I especially hate to *work* on a fish—with someone looking over my shoulder. I invariably experience this in a Rotation. However, at odd hours I'll often check out pools that are usually fished in Rotation. If nobody is fishing the pool I'll sit on the bank and postpone fishing as long as I can, to further rest the salmon, which is usually until another angler shows up and forces me to fish before he does.

Given the nature of wet-fly fishing you should never get into the water downstream of another angler in the same pool, unless he has at least 100 yards of fishable water, or it's getting so late in the day that he won't be able to fish down through. If there's a reasonable amount of space or a dramatic difference between the top and bottom parts of a pool, sometimes I'll get in and fish the tail while an angler is up at the head. Matalik is a perfect example of such a pool (refer to fig. 7-1). Many people just fish the run at the top, then leave when they get down to the slack water in the gut. If there's no distinct difference between the head and tail of a pool, however, always fish behind (upstream of) the other angler. Also, avoid crowding or being crowded by other anglers.

Dry-fly fishing is a little trickier, because you—and others—are so often casting to visible fish, or just working over a small, specific area to see if you can raise a fish. Anglers in a Rotation often use dry flies, and the same rules apply. Because a dry fly's effective float is so much shorter than a wet fly's swing, you can usually make three or four casts with the dry fly for every one made by the wet-fly angler. But you have to move at about the same pace.

If you're unsure of a dry-fly angler's intentions, don't be afraid to ask if he's fishing through or just working that little area. Give him room if he wants to fish his way down. But if he's fishing upstream, and you're wet-fly fishing downstream, you more or less have the right-of-way—because that's the standard in fishing.

I almost always feel free to fish to salmon I spot unless it's clear that they'll soon be covered by an angler working his way downstream. For instance, let's say there's a narrow, deep channel containing salmon right below a road, and there's no other decent-looking water from the channel to the far bank. An angler fishing down through the channel (from the far bank toward the road) has the right to cover the fish first—even though he may not even know they're there. But if that angler is 100 yards upstream (or even much less, if it's obvious he can't or won't be able to cover the water near the fish), I consider the visible fish something that I found and am entitled to try. This is sometimes a real judgment call; always weigh the situation.

If and when an angler near you hooks a fish, reel up quickly and back out of the way so as not to interfere with the battle. If you hook a fish, holler "Fish on!" and expect anyone else in the pool to clear the way for you. Catching a salmon is a special event, and everyone fishing the same pool is usually happy to help you land it. By the same token you should always offer—or at least be prepared—to help someone else land his fish.

Be careful wading water you don't know. One of the most common beginner's errors made by trout anglers is wading too far out into the fast riffle or run at the head of a pool. This can disturb the salmon and ruin the fishing for others. Also, when you cross the river, make sure to do so in a place that isn't being fished, and make as little commotion as possible when wading.

Anglers who are wading and those fishing from boats don't *have* to be in conflict, but it often ends up that way. Boaters too often fish—or even just float by—in front of waders. Because anglers in boats often park midstream and fish drops off both sides, they sometimes think nothing of invading a wader's territory on the often shaky premise that they're covering different water, and from an angle that the wader couldn't duplicate even if he tried. But if anglers in a boat are overlapping at all with a wading angler who was there first, they're in the wrong.

Boaters, including recreationists who aren't fishing, often ignore a cardinal rule of etiquette: Pass *behind* anglers rather than over the water they're fishing. It's always nice when someone shows manners enough to follow this rule; still, the boaters rarely hurt your chances irrevocably. Salmon are pretty oblivious to boats traveling nearby, although they always move if you drift directly over them in anything but very deep water. However, traveling fish tend to get nervous and speed up for a while when a boat passes, and fish holding in shallow water often move quite a distance from their lies when disturbed by a boat. Those fish almost always return to their original lies, and they're just as apt to take a fly as they were before they were disturbed.

Ethical issues are much more complicated than those of etiquette, because they're more than merely practical strictures for getting along or even for practicing sound conservation. Ethics involve an individual's values. They're about an angler's understanding and endorsement of the concept of Fair Chase, and the desire to capture and release—or kill—salmon as humanely as possible.

This is the real-world difference between fishing and merely gathering food. It's also the difference between the ritual taking of salmon in a clean and simple way and the turning of salmon into living props for egotistical stunts.

Fair Chase is the philosophy of accepting restrictions that help level the playing field, giving salmon—or deer, or partridge—a chance to elude capture by craft, agility, or strength. The ethical angler doesn't merely want to get a salmon; he wants to catch one in a way that demands skill and gives the fish a chance to win. The laws of Fair Chase change, and there's no universal agreement on them, but they can be described as sportsmanship. Just where an individual draws the line—does Fair Chase demand the use of barbless hooks, or is that just an additional flourish for anglers seeking a greater challenge?—defines the nature and quality of his ethics.

The concept of sportsmanship evolved from the Anglo-Saxon notion of the gentleman—the secular equivalent of a priest, who adhered to a code of conduct, or ethics. This code eventually influenced law. At their best, laws are both practical *and* ethical. For instance, restricting all Atlantic salmon angling in eastern Canada to fly fishing (a radical idea, when you think about it) not only mandates that anglers fish in the most sporting way, but also curbs the potential devastation of the resource by anglers using gear that can be much more lethal in unscrupulous hands.

Many years ago I went to the Matane River with Richard Franklin, Jim Emery, and another fishing buddy, Greg Hubert. The water was medium low, and the fish were pooled up. On the third morning of the trip we all went up to a holding pool, Gaudreau. There were many fish lying in the pool's streamy tail, clearly visible in 2 feet of water. Although these fish wouldn't move to a fly, their presence suggested that there might be fish up at the head of the pool, in water too swift and deep for visibility.

Richard and Greg, an accomplished fisherman who was relatively new to salmon fishing, went up to the head. I stayed down below to fish the deeper portion of the tailout. After failing to move a fish, Greg decided to try a sinking line, the theory being that he could in this way drift the fly closer to fish that were obviously in no mood to rise to the surface. Sinking lines weren't illegal, and over the previous days we had heard more than once about some fishermen from New Jersey who were catching a remarkable number of salmon on nymphs and sinking lines.

To an experienced trout fisherman like Greg, this strategy seemed intelligent. But I had fished for salmon long enough to know that using sinking lines on summer-run fish in rivers running at low levels was a sure ticket to foul-hooking fish. I had learned this the hard way myself years earlier, when I switched to a fast-sinking line in the hope of tempting a huge salmon lying in very deep water under Heppel Bridge Pool on the Matapedia. When I reached the fish, I actually felt one cast rake its flank; this harassment caused the salmon to break water and bolt upstream.

As soon as Greg got out a decent amount of line, he hooked a fish that screamed straight downstream toward me. A few moments later the fly pulled out. I hollered up to Greg, and he replied that the fish had taken as soon as he changed to a sinking line. Two or three casts later, Greg was fast to another salmon. This fish behaved in much the same way, turning downstream and racing as fast as it could. This convinced me that Greg had foul-hooked the two fish (they fight differently than when hooked in the mouth), and that he could probably hook 5 or 7 or even 20 more with no trouble. Greg is an ethical, principled fisherman, and he soon realized that the fish had indeed been foul-hooked. We had a bankside powwow and all agreed not to use sinking lines.

The following year, a large sign appeared in the parking pullout for the heavily fished holding pool Grand Tamagodie advising anglers that the "Code d'Éthique" prohibited the use of sinking lines (even if the law did not). I hoped that the great nymph-fishing experts from New Jersey took heed.

In the previous chapter, I wrote briefly about the curious "viewing box," a periscope in reverse. Stick it into a clean river and you can see clearly for up to about 20 yards. Many accomplished, ethical anglers use these instruments on clear rivers, but they have always rubbed me the wrong way. I like looking into them, but I don't like using them to locate salmon while fishing. This is because, in my estimation, the more we rely on our God-given senses (combined with intelligence and experience), the closer we come to matching the definition of Fair Chase. Of course earlier in this book I stressed the importance of wearing quality polarized sunglasses to help spot fish, and I admit that I fish with rods made from space-age synthetics. Angling ethics is a search for general standards, not an attempt to define *the* singular ethically correct way to fish.

Along those same lines, I used to be adamant about not "spotting" for my companions—or having them spot for me. At the time I felt that having your buddy climb a tree and tell you what kind of a swing or float you were getting over a fish was somehow cheating. I believed that catching a fish ought to be a one-on-one, man-against-fish challenge. But fishing with guides over the years, and thinking about the cooperative and social nature of the hunt, eventually changed my mind. There may be no group experience in which participants feel greater commonality, solidarity, and companionship than the hunt. To me, that supersedes the one-on-one sensibility.

In trying to define the foundation of angling ethics, I also mentioned the ethical angler's desire to catch fish in as humane a way as possible. This area sometimes overlaps with the notion of Fair Chase, which is fine, but can also contradict it, which is bad. The more Fair Chase becomes a way to demonstrate skill and prowess, the further it may depart from the equally important ethical concept of humane treatment of the quarry.

Most anglers will tell you that salmon in low water during a heat wave are very difficult to catch, succumbing only to the smallest of flies fished with the greatest of care. But the downside of this otherwise great challenge is that as the water creeps above 70 degrees Fahrenheit, the fish become increasingly stressed. At such times, hooking and landing a salmon—particularly on the light equipment appropriate for the conditions—may excessively tax a fish, leaving it susceptible to disease and less fit to endure the rigors of spawning and recuperating. I don't know of any scientific research on this subject comparable with the work done by the ASF on the survival and spawning success rate among caught-and-released salmon (the study showed that catching and releasing salmon properly did not endanger them or prevent them from spawning), but I'm assured the concern is legitimate. It would be impossible to write and enforce laws governing angling during hot weather, of course, although rivers are often closed when they become dangerously low and warm. Much of the time this issue is up to angler discretion—and ethics.

Recently an accomplished, dedicated angler-celebrity with a jet-set lifestyle excitedly told me about his first salmon fishing trip. Naturally he had been invited to an exclusive camp on terrific water, where there was little doubt he would add the Atlantic salmon to the impressive list of exotic gamefish he'd caught. The guy caught salmon, and he was particularly proud of a 12-pounder taken on the lightest rod made—a wisp of graphite designed to cast a *1*-weight line on tiny trout streams.

I told him what I thought—that fishing with such light tackle is a stunt that unduly strains fish; that salmon ought to be fished with appropriate tackle, because it subdues them relatively quickly and efficiently without overpowering them. It's the most humane way to catch salmon. My friend was taken aback, and he quickly explained that he had indeed fought and landed the fish briskly, and it appeared none the worse for the wear when he released it.

I don't doubt that that's true, but it wouldn't always be. And to me, the risk of hurting a fish's chance of survival far outweighs the value of the accomplishment. I simply have no desire to perform such a stunt, even though I grew up under the influence of the angling icon and stuntman extraordinaire Lee Wulff. But it's important to remember that Lee performed many of his feats with the higher purpose of defining and demonstrating the relatively new sport of light-tackle angling, thereby raising in our consciousness the very idea of Fair Chase. And unlike many of his successors, Lee was an expert at landing big fish with wispy rods.

Thankfully, anglers as a group have evolved beyond an obsession with light tackle. The most reliable guideline in our ethics is a basic sense of appropriateness. You can catch a 12-pound salmon on a 1-weight rod, just as you can free-climb a rock escarpment with an infant strapped to your back. Either action simply shows a basic insensitivity to the well-being of another creature.

There's always an ego component in fishing, and most of the accomplished anglers I know are competitive and keenly aware of how the proverbial "other guy" is doing. I'm the same way myself more often than I'd like to admit. But our basic appreciation of the resource can be

Playing a big one on the Grand Cascapedia River, Quebec (Photo: Val Atkinson)

damaged when we become too taken with the challenge of catching fish. One of the wisest remarks I ever read or heard suggested that it is unseemly to take too seriously the act of catching a fish. Trying to balance this with the legitimate goal of becoming a skilled, experienced angler can be difficult.

In Canada, the province-by-province regulations pertaining to catching and releasing or keeping fish puts some serious constraints on the angler. Although the specific laws vary, they all ensure that if the fishing is really hot, you aren't going to be on the water for very long. Even in New Brunswick, a province where the MSW fishery is exclusively catch-and-release, the law demands that you quit after releasing four fish. On the Grand Cascapedia in Quebec you're allowed to kill or release one MSW salmon per day, and then you're done.

Some of these regulations embody a serious conflict. The sporting angler wants to fish more than he wants to kill or even release salmon. Having to quit on the rare day when the fishing is great contradicts the very concept of fishing for sport. In fact, Chris von Strasser gave up his rights to a prime-time week on the Grand Cascapedia because he got tired of going out every morning, catching his one salmon, then having to hang around the camp, reading or eating, for the rest of the day. The fishing was so good that Chris didn't do any of it.

Most anglers would give their eyeteeth to have this "problem." Likewise, there's something so glorious about catching a salmon that quitting for the rest of the day sometimes seems like an appropriate act of appreciation. And as most public-water salmon anglers will tell you, taking off a good part of the day after you've been up at dawn and fishing until sunset for a few days is a pleasure that you really savor.

The general laws are meant to support the conservation effort. Ultimately fishing is disturbing to fish, and you and I both know that there are anglers out there who would gladly catch 4 or 6 or 15 salmon a day, just as there are children—and adults—who will eat chocolate cake until its delicious taste becomes meaningless. It doesn't matter that these fish will be released; there's something creepy about overusing any resource, about lacking the self-control to pull back and say, "The river's been kind today. I think I'll give the fish a rest and just sit on this rock for the rest of the afternoon and watch the water."

Fish hogs diminish the opportunities for other anglers, particularly less skilled ones, whose chances of catching a salmon considerably increase when the law demands that everyone quit after catching one or two salmon.

Then again, I remember days when . . .

Well, you can see that I'm really torn on this one. But that's ethics for you.

Remember to treat those parr like the tiny, living jewels that they are.

Good-bye, and tight lines!

The author's fine catch-before-release from Le Panier (Photo: Richard Franklin)

APPENDIX 1

Province-by-Province Guide

This appendix is intended to give a broad overview of the regulations and opportunities governing Atlantic salmon fishing in the state of Maine and in eastern Canada. Salmon are an intensively managed resource, and the laws regulating fishing may vary from one river to another—even within the same province. For instance, on many rivers in New Brunswick, a licensed guide may fish for the sport who has engaged him—but any fish he lands counts in the *sport's* bag limit. Regulations are also subject to change as conditions dictate. For instance, during extreme low-water periods, entire rivers may be closed to angling.

For such reasons, it is very important for the prospective angler to have good, reliable information when planning and taking a trip. Advance knowledge is a critical component in Atlantic salmon fishing— more so than in most other kinds of fishing. The traditional primary source for such information is the summary published in booklet form by Maine and each Canadian province. However, regulatory nuances are often so complex that it always pays to double-check on specifics (such as the use of treble hooks, which are often forbidden in some places) with knowledgeable on-river sources.

Some of the better sources of information on both rivers and regulations are now available on the Internet. This is an invaluable, cheap, quick way to gather information and to communicate with official authorities as well as other salmon anglers. Using even the most basic browse-and-search techniques you'll find Web sites, bulletin boards, and chat rooms dedicated to salmon. If you don't have the equipment or experience to surf the Internet, here are some specific Web sites that a computer-literate friend can use to help you. The province of Quebec has a comprehensive Web site available at http://www.quebectel. com/saumonquebec/anglais/index.htm (the "anglais" is for text in English). The Francophone arm of the ASF, the Fédération Québécoise pour le Saumon Atlantique, has a Web site at http://www.FQSA @qu-bec.com. You can also reach the Atlantic Salmon Federation via e-mail at asfpub@nbnet.nb.ca. Other web sites are appearing on almost a daily basis.

Other good sources of information include the *Atlantic Salmon Journal* (a quarterly magazine that is free with ASF membership), regional fish and game departments, tourism offices, camp owners and operators, and commercially published books.

Because so many parts of salmon country are remote, finding reliable local contacts, from tackle shops to provincial agencies, isn't always easy. But it is always worth the effort.

Keep in mind that bag limits operate on the tag system. When you buy a license, you're issued a number of tags that resemble hospital bracelets made of thick plastic. Each tag has an ID number and provincial identification. If you choose to kill a salmon, you must immediately attach one of the tags that you received with your license. The tag can be slipped through the gills and mouth, although most anglers make an incision near the tail of the fish and slip the tag through there. Once closed, the tags cannot—and should not—be removed until the fish is about to be cooked. Also remember that if and when you use up all your tags, you must stop fishing. That is, you can't fill your annual bag limit and then fish on a catch-and-release basis. *Your license becomes invalid once you use up all your tags.*

All the dollar figures in this appendix, with the exception of those for the state of Maine, are given in Canadian dollars. Generally, the U.S. dollar is worth about 20 percent more than its Canadian counterpart.

MAINE

Almost all the salmon fishing done in Maine takes place on the Penobscot River near Bangor, during a season that begins on May 1 and ends on October 15. Thanks to Veasie Dam, the Penobscot isn't subject to the dramatic water-level fluctuations and discoloration that free-flowing rivers suffer early in the season. The other Maine salmon rivers are small, with modest numbers of fish. Unless I had some special "inside" information, I wouldn't plan a trip to anyplace other than the Penobscot.

> **License fee:** Resident, $15; nonresident, $40—for the required Atlantic salmon license. A standard fishing license is required in addition to the special salmon license.

> **Bag limits:** *All* salmon fishing in Maine is catch-and-release.

> **Contacts:** The Atlantic Salmon Authority, Bangor, Maine, 207-941-4449, 207-941-4443 (fax).

> **Recommended rivers:** Penobscot.

NEW BRUNSWICK

The noteworthy feature of New Brunswick regulations is that they require nonresidents to fish with licensed guides. Thus this is not a province suited to just knocking around, looking for a fishing opportunity. Visiting anglers almost always plan their trips through camps, or on the advice of fellow anglers who have had good luck hiring guides with access to good salmon water. It's always a good idea to get references from camps and guides if you picked them cold.

New Brunswick has a wide variety of water that, while not exactly public, is leased by camps or guides and thus available to their clients. It also features "Crown Reserve" water, which is only available to provincial residents.

License and access fees: Because of the system requiring the use of a guide, the only fee for nonresidents salmon fishers in New Brunswick is the cost of a license, which ranges from $25 (three consecutive days) to $100 (entire season). A season license for residents costs $16.

Bag limits: New Brunswick, the pioneer province in salmon conservation, allows only catch-and-release fishing for MSW salmon. An angler may hook and release up to four salmon (including grilse) a day, unless he has already killed and tagged his daily limit of two grilse. Officially, a grilse is a fish less than 63 centimeters (24.8 inches) long from the tip of its nose to the fork (center) of its tail. (This definition is used by all the Canadian provinces.) The season bag limit ranges from two fish (tags) for a nonresident angler fishing with a three-day license to a maximum of eight fish per season for residents and visitors alike.

Special regulations: The use of treble hooks (such as those sometimes used on tube flys, or with Waddington shanks) is forbidden.

Contacts: New Brunswick Department of Economic Development and Tourism, 1-800-561-0123. Web site: http://www.gov.nb.ca/tourism.

Recommended rivers: The Miramichi drainage produces more salmon and offers more public fishing opportunities than any other river system in North America, and it has a staggering variety of water types. Other excellent rivers include the Restigouche, St. John, Nepisiguit, Renous, and Tobique.

QUEBEC

For anglers the distinguishing features of this province are the complexity of its regulations combined with the problems posed to English-speaking visitors within a bilingual locale. The rivers of Quebec are micromanaged, offering an angler a bewildering number of ways to get onto the water, including a variety of telephone "lottery" drawings in which callers can reserve water in advance on a first-come, first-served basis on specified days during the off season.

Quebec is rich in public salmon fishing opportunities, ranging from the superb angling available on strictly controlled—and relatively expensive—waters such as the Glen Emma section of the Matapedia (about $450 Canadian per day for nonresidents) to the quality fishing available for the cost of a license and a day permit (about $50 per day) on many rivers, including the Matane, York, and Bonaventure.

Quebec allows anglers to kill MSW salmon (one per day and up to, but no more than, eight per season) as well as grilse. This year Quebec offers a novel season catch-and-release license available for under $10.

License and access fees: Resident (entire season) $40; nonresident, $100. Shorter-term licenses are available as well, including a one-day, one-tag license for residents and non-residents.

Bag limits: One MSW and one grilse per day, provided that the grilse is caught first. If the salmon is caught first, the angler must quit fishing for the day. An angler who catches and kills a grilse first may continue to fish and is allowed to keep or release an MSW salmon as well.

Special regulations: The abundance of management systems on Quebec rivers makes it imperative that you check with local authorities. The upside of this is that there is a strong, helpful infrastructure of management on most Quebec rivers.

Contacts: Quebec Department of Tourism, 1-800-363-7777. The FQSA in Montreal, 1-888-SAUMONS.

Recommended rivers: The Matapedia, Matane, York, Ste. Marguerite, Ste. Jean, Bonaventure, Grand and Petite Cascapedia, Dartmouth, and Patapedia.

NOVA SCOTIA

This province has a great commitment to the spirit of public fishing. All that either a resident or nonresident angler needs in order to fish for salmon is a valid fishing license. Recently Nova Scotia has also embraced catch-and-release-only regulations for MSW salmon.

License and access fees: Nonresidents pay $112.35 for an annual license, or may buy a seven-day license for $42.80. A resident license costs $26.75.

Bag limits: You may catch and release up to four salmon (including grilse) unless you have already killed the daily limit of two grilse. The season bag limit for all anglers is eight grilse (tags provided).

Special regulations: Nova Scotia law requires all anglers to complete the stub that comes attached to every license as part of its management plan.

Contacts: Nova Scotia Department of Fisheries, Halifax; Nova Scotia Department of Fisheries, Pictou; Nova Scotia Tourism, Halifax, 1-800-565-6096, 902-424-2668 (fax). Web site: http://explore.gov.ns.ca/virtualns.

Recommended rivers: The LaHave, Musquodoboit, St. Mary's Liscomb, Gold, Clyde, and Medway. The Margaree, and nearby waters including the West and East Rivers and the river Phillip, offer outstanding fall fishing.

NEWFOUNDLAND AND LABRADOR

An aggressive campaign to drastically curtail commercial interceptory fisheries in this critical travel corridor has turned Newfoundland and Labrador into hot destinations for many knowledgeable salmon anglers. If the province were as accessible and well known as Quebec or New Brunswick, it would probably be overrun with these anglers. Like New Brunswick, this province requires nonresidents to fish with guides on salmon rivers. But unlike New Brunswick, very little of Newfoundland and Labrador is leased or privately held water. Thus an angler needn't worry about the amount or quality of water available to his guide or outfitter.

License and access fees: It's a straightforward $20 for the resident, $50 for the nonresident. This province also offers a quaint "family" license for a 50 percent surcharge. This license allows everyone in the family to fish, although the bag limit is the same as for an individual license.

Bag limits: Newfoundland has also embraced catch-and-release for MSW salmon, allowing anglers to catch up to four salmon a day and to kill up to two grilse a day. In Labrador, anglers are allowed to kill only one MSW salmon (over 63 centimeters) per *year.* The provincial bag limit for the year is six fish.

Special regulations: Newfoundland has innovative programs that open some rivers to early catch-and-release angling, and turn other rivers into catch-and-release fisheries once certain catch-and-retain quotas have been achieved.

Contacts: The Department of Tourism, Culture and Recreation in St. John's, Newfoundland, 1-800-563-6353, 709-729-0057 (fax), bmetcalfe@tourism.gov.nf.ca (email), publishes one of the best hunting and fishing guides I've seen, complete with an index of outfitters.

Recommended rivers: The Exploits River in Newfoundland produces annual runs of 10,000-plus fish. Some of the other standouts include the Humber, Great and Little Codroy Rivers, Portland Creek River, and River of Ponds. In Labrador, the superstars are the Eagle and Pinware.

PRINCE EDWARD ISLAND

Although it isn't a popular or well-publicized destination, PEI contains a number of salmon rivers, and many of them feature a special, catch-and-release late season running from the middle of September through October.

License and access fees: The annual salmon license for all anglers is a bargain at $9.35, but it must be used in conjunction with a trout angling license, which costs nonresidents $18.70. At that price, the license holder's spouse and dependents also get to fish free for two weeks from the license's date of issue. The resident trout license costs $9.35.

Bag limits: One grilse per day, seven allowed during the season. Catch-and-release anglers may release two salmon per day.

Special regulations: See regulations booklet for specific opening and closing dates.

Contacts: Department of Environmental Resources Fish and Wildlife Division Office, Charlottetown, 1-800-463-4734.

Recommended rivers: The Morell, Valleyfield, Dunk, Midgell, and Naufrage are among PEI's salmon rivers.

APPENDIX II

Catch Statistics

Catch Statistics 1991–1996											
	1991		1992		1993		1994		1995		1996	
Sport Catch Totals	Grilse	Salmon	Grilse	Salmon	Grilse	Salmon	Grilse	Salmon	Grilse	Salmon	Grilse	Salmon
New Brunswick Rivers												
Big Salmon	0	0	36	45	0	0	0	0	closed to	angling		
Cains	530	370	608	451	757	486	120	42	20	20		
Kennebecasis	30	20	144	90	111	160	12	6	closed to	angling		
Little S.W. Miramichi	1,000	510	2,701	718	2,383	645	2,868	821	770	210		
N.W. Miramichi	1,320	530	4,432	906	3,973	987	3,560	1,039	1,110	320		
S.W. Miramichi	7,070	2,880	14,518	6,234	10,239	4,020	9,731	5,213	5,130	2,200		
Nepisiguit	850300	300	1,130	270	555	258	450	250	450	300		
Restigouche (N.B. Portion)	1,987	2,181	3,999	3,351	2,472	1,541	3,942	3,016	1,235	1,926		
St. John	850	340	1,538	1,263	665	582	307	130	closed to	angling		
Tobique	760	650	1,442	1,045	1,265	638	260	265	closed to	angling		
Totals	14,397	7,781	30,548	14,373	22,420	9,317	21,250	10,782	8,715	4,976		
Nova Scotia												
La Have	227	125	1,136	184	1,121	237	157	117	611	217	1,535	331
Margaree	558	1,755	673	1,973	735	1,051	434	1,466	323	1,040	1,164	1,856
Medway	48	48	533	45	280	63	76	42	123	40	507	92
St. Mary's	762	278	333	165	864	315	44	30	560	131	627	190
Stewiacke	143	40	0	0	-	-	closed to	angling	closed to	angling	closed to	angling
Totals	1,738	2,246	2,675	2,367	3,000	3,000	711	1,655	1,617	1,428	3,833	2,469
Prince Edward Island												
Morell River	1,690	164	0	NA	NA	NA	342	155	603	98	697	161

Statistics were compiled courtesy of the N.B. Department of Natural Resources, the Department of Fisheries and Oceans, Québec Ministère de l'Environment et de la Faune, and the Maine Atlantic Salmon Authority. Statistics for New Brunswick rivers for 1996 are not available.

Catch Statistics 1991–1996											
	1991		**1992**		**1993**		**1994**		**1995**		**1996**
Sport Catch Totals	Grilse	Salmon	Grilse	Salmon	Grilse	Salmon	Grilse	Salmon	Grilse	Salmon	Grilse	Salmon
Newfoundland & Labrador												
Big	4	1	25	76	135	5	772	117	880	98	97	13
Conne	108	-	329	-	329	0	closed to	angling	closed to	angling	closed to	angling
Crabbes	105	9	289	88	150	24	211	45	31	32	N/A	N/A
Eagle	833	18	670	151	1,595	107	2,012	381	1,825	371	716	163
East Big	141	0	434	40	500	30	395	34	267	29	N/A	N/A
Exploits	1,056	-	1,408	-	4,635	59	4,217	30	2,867	72	1,915	111
Gambo	802	-	479	-	1,012	5	1,012	4	820	4	1,755	0
Gander	1,180	-	1,268	-	3,221	92	2,571	39	3,210	74	3,009	73
Garnish	491	-	300	-	1,093	5	692	2	1,217	5	1,374	3
Grandy	419	-	497	-	713	31	431	10	435	1	566	4
Humber	1,431	11	2,428	177	2,807	125	2,011	166	2,530	233	2,448	237
Hunt	-	-	29	22	68	19	121	33	261	58	10	10
Pinware	-	-	666	229	990	225	441	107	749	268	N/A	N/A
Serpentine	132	46	266	89	263	63	136	93	145	133	N/A	N/A
Terra Nova	448	-	409	-	1,053	62	1,000	44	828	72	1,056	113
Totals	7,148	85	9,497	872	18,564	852	16,130	1,105	16,065	1,450	12,946	727
Quebec												
Bonaventure	399	799	477	927	536	767	584	1,134	164	870	321	370
Dartmouth	130	287	141	390	267	473	202	588	35	319	152	347
De la Chaloupe	59	74	62	48	102	18	156	89	59	64	126	98
Etamamiou	324	40	319	82	414	136	318	82	298	63	344	82
George	347	279	85	84	98	170	-	-	246	242	120	90
Grand Cascapedia	69	826	125	929	105	953	129	1,127	38	920	79	1,081
Jupiter	59	286	65	145	143	54	217	14	119	30	279	39
Matane	372	482	645	680	712	620	479	602	302	277	524	514
Matapedia	521	940	693	693	735	505	822	917	337	829	721	922
Moisie	41	2,249	32	2,167	17	1,678	33	1,347	14	717	29	1,130
Natashquan	411	453	694	407	346	344	442	322	280	469	351	307
Quelle	26	38	128	60	18	29	119	18	72	71	230	60
St. Paul	350	18	474	52	401	86	302	57	292	29	319	67
Ste. Anne	100	499	78	211	99	147	133	347	44	168	48	184
Ste. Jean (Gaspe)	139	507	289	658	314	514	248	586	80	420	151	368
Ste. Marguerite	219	351	200	403	117	95	61	76	52	122	140	161
Trinite	345	128	217	156	171	57	183	35	100	108	182	65
Whale	2	38	-	-	15	15	-	-	41	15	17	23
York	118	566	329	730	329	620	261	750	68	484	215	744
Totals	4,031	8,860	5,053	9,095	4,939	7,281	4,689	8,091	2,641	6,217	4,348	6,652
Maine												
Dennys	7	1	5	7	3	1	33		20		400	
Machias	0	0	3	7	0	0	5		5		31	
E. Machias	5	0	6	3	0	3	12		22		10	
Narraguagus	22	4	17	45	7	20	20		23		21	
Penobscot	170	210	153	344	124	450	182		300		60	
Saco	0	0	0	0	6	6	1		0		0	
Sheepscot	4	0	7	0	9	5	6		0		0	
All others	6	1	11	12	1	1	9		0		20	
Totals	214	216	202	418	150	486	262		370		542	

INDEX